Praise for
The Power of a Half Hour

"*The Power of a Half Hour* is full of unique, practical, and God-inspired truths to keep your time focused on all that God has called you to do. If you apply these principles, I believe it will bring renewed purpose and inspiration to your life."

—JOYCE MEYER, Bible teacher and best-selling author

"Before reading this book, I never thought of seeing thirty minutes as a power-packed opportunity to improve my life. Pastor Barnett's half-hour power principles have helped me strengthen my faith, become more productive, and connect with those I love with more intentionality. This book is as inspirational as it is practical, and I plan to use it as an integral part of my staff development program."

—LYSA TERKEURST, *New York Times* best-selling author and president of Proverbs 31 Ministries

"Tommy Barnett inspires people to be bold witnesses and fulfill Christ's commission. He accomplishes much for the kingdom. After reading this dynamic book, you'll understand why. His concept of 'thirty minutes' can help you make the most of each day—in many areas—and enable you to have a positive influence on others."

—JAMES ROBISON, founder and president, LIFE Outreach International

"Pastor Tommy Barnett is a hero of mine. He is a father in the faith, a man of great conviction, and a visionary who has changed the lives of many—including my own. His grasp on the Word of God and its power to radically alter the course of your life will bless and inspire you. Allow the deep revelations and years of wisdom from this man of God to impart health and life into your faith journey."

—BRIAN HOUSTON, senior pastor, Hillsong Church

THE

POWER

OF A

HALF

HOUR

TOMMY BARNETT

THE
POWER
OF A
HALF
HOUR

Take Back Your Life Thirty Minutes at a Time

WATERBROOK
PRESS

THE POWER OF A HALF HOUR
PUBLISHED BY WATERBROOK PRESS
12265 Oracle Boulevard, Suite 200
Colorado Springs, Colorado 80921

All Scripture quotations, unless otherwise indicated, are from the New Revised Standard Version of the Bible, copyright © 1989 by the Division of Christian Education of the National Council of the Churches of Christ in the USA. Used by permission. All rights reserved. Scripture quotations marked (KJV) are taken from the King James Version. Scripture quotations marked (NLT) are taken from the Holy Bible, New Living Translation, copyright © 1996, 2004, 2007. Used by permission of Tyndale House Publishers Inc., Carol Stream, Illinois 60188. All rights reserved.

Details in some anecdotes and stories have been changed to protect the identities of the persons involved.

Hardcover ISBN 978-0-307-73184-5
eBook ISBN 978-0-307-73185-2

Personal Power of a Half Hour Action Plan and Small-Group Study Guide prepared by Stephen Sorenson.

Cover design by Brand Navigation

Published in association with the literary agency of Fedd & Company, Inc., P.O. Box 341973, Austin, TX 78734.

Published in the United States by WaterBrook Multnomah, an imprint of the Crown Publishing Group, a division of Random House LLC, New York, a Penguin Random House Company.

WATERBROOK and its deer colophon are registered trademarks of Random House LLC.

Library of Congress Cataloging-in-Publication Data
Barnett, Tommy.
  The power of a half hour : take back your life 30 minutes at a time / Tommy Barnett.—First Edition.
   pages cm
  Includes bibliographical references.
  ISBN 978-0-307-73184-5—ISBN 9780307731852 1. Time management—Religious aspects—Christianity. I. Title.
  BV4598.5.B37 2013
  248.4—dc23

            2013029666

Printed in the United States of America
2013—First Edition

10 9 8 7 6 5 4 3 2 1

SPECIAL SALES
Most WaterBrook Multnomah books are available at special quantity discounts when purchased in bulk by corporations, organizations, and special-interest groups. Custom imprinting or excerpting can also be done to fit special needs. For information, please e-mail SpecialMarkets@WaterBrookMultnomah.com or call 1-800-603-7051.

I dedicate this book to my administrative assistant of forty years, Lynn Lane, who helped me live my life by schedule and the half-hour principle.

CONTENTS

THE POWER OF A HALF HOUR

My name is Tommy Barnett.

I'm a pastor and have devoted my entire adult life to helping people connect with God and find better ways to live. I could fill up this book and more with all kinds of spiritual and practical ideas about what works in life and what doesn't. I think it would be good stuff, but I have one practical idea that I know from my own experience rises far above all the others.

I admit it's not an overly unique concept, like the invention of the Internet, for example. However, it's an idea that has helped me realize success and great satisfaction in all aspects of my personal and professional life. I mean everything—from personal goals and dreams to marriage to raising a family to relationships to work.

> I believe the idea can change your life,
> though, as it has changed mine.

Most importantly, it has helped me serve God and others more effectively.

Trust me, my idea is not rocket science; in fact, it's so simple that anyone can understand and benefit from it.

I believe the idea can change your life, though, as it has changed mine.

I call it *the power of a half hour.*

Many people think of a half hour as a minimal or meaningless gap in time, downtime to catch your breath between periods of major effort. But the truth is your half hours can determine the difference between success and failure. Your half hours direct and shape your future.

You can literally change your world in thirty minutes. In the same way that your effect on the world is felt one life at a time, so is that effect delivered through the careful and thoughtful investment of your half hours. The beauty of this reality is that anyone can do it. You don't need a PhD, and you don't need a life coach to pull it off. All you need is to accept the idea, have a clear sense of your God-given purpose, examine your activity patterns, sensitize yourself to your time choices, and start taking advantage of the power of a half hour.

Every half hour in your day is a power-loaded resource. Your choice of how to spend those minutes is the focus of this book, which I intend to make a practical conversation about a resource that we misunderstand, abuse, take for granted, and ignore.

I want to help you become the person God intends you to be and accomplish His plans for your life. And in order to do that, you need to use your small increments of time wisely—not just the big slices of time that are devoted to both routine daily activities and major life events.

I agree with Harvey Mackay who said, "Time is free, but it's priceless. You can't own it, but you can use it. You can't keep it, but you can spend it. Once you've lost it, you can never get it back."[1]

I know that it's not easy to find even a "free" hour in the world we live in. I also have learned that it's difficult to accomplish a great deal in a quarter hour—especially if you need to communicate graciously and genuinely with another person within that time frame. But a half hour—*it works!*

CLAIMING THE POWER OF A HALF HOUR

Here's how we will approach turning your half hours into life-changing blocks of time. In the seven parts of this book, I will outline how seizing the power of a half hour can make such a difference in these major areas:

- Impact
- Purpose and goals
- Faith
- Character
- Dreams
- Relationships
- Advancing God's kingdom

To help you remember key themes in this book, each chapter contains a *Half-Hour Power Principle.*

By the way, researchers tell us that most people never finish reading the books they start. Because I think there's too much helpful information in these pages for you to abandon the content before you get to the end, let me suggest that you do four simple but practical things as you read this book.

First, read the book in half-hour spaces in your schedule. Each of the chapters in the book is short enough to read easily in a half hour. You might want to have more than one block during a day when you read the book, but start this practice as you engage with this book. In addition, at the back of this book you will find a Personal Power of a Half Hour Action Plan. This plan is set up to help you, over a thirty-day period, fully incorporate *The Power of a Half Hour* concepts into all major areas of your life. You have heard that it takes about a month to establish a new habit? I urge you to use this thirty-day plan to make the power of a half hour a habit you will never break!

Second, if something strikes you as personally helpful, jot down notes about changes you need to make. Too often we are so intent on getting through a book that we forget some of the useful insights or challenges it provided.

Third, pray that God will help you to implement the things you discover in these pages (or in your related reflections) that will improve your life experience.

Fourth, and finally, express a commitment to someone you know and trust that you are going to integrate these simple changes into your lifestyle. Ask that person to check up on you once or twice a month to see how intentional you are being with your half hours. That simple act of accountability will help prevent the reading of this book from being just another helpful but forgotten task. (You may also wish to find mutual encouragement in learning the half-hour concepts by attending a small-group discussion. A guide for such a study is included at the end of the book.)

I've been practicing these principles so long that I can now say I am a product of my half hours. I don't always get it right, but I'm very much aware of the gift of life and the value of time. My half hours—the ones I carefully plan, as well as the unplanned ones I discover—are committed to doing His will in my life because I want to serve our God and others.

> I've been practicing these principles
> so long that I can now say I am
> a product of my half hours.

If you get your half hours right, God will not only change your life but also use you to alter the lives of the people and organizations you influence. I sincerely believe the future is not going to be defined by those who rely on their intelligence, their talent, or their good looks. Instead, the future is dependent on the choices made by God's people in the time that He has placed at our disposal.

Part 1

The Power of a Half Hour to

IMPACT YOUR LIFE

CHANGE YOUR DESTINY

Half-Hour Power Principle:
Thirty minutes can wreck or redeem a life.

Wonderful and bad things can happen in a mere eighteen hundred seconds. Just ask a man I know named Carl Schultz.[2] He experienced the power of a half hour in extremes.

Carl is a born salesman. From his very youngest years, he displayed unusual persuasive skills, figuring out ways to make money by selling things to his friends and, later on, to adults. It is a talent that has served him well.

In the early eighties Carl tired of selling for the benefit of other people and decided to begin his own company. He started a firm that sold bullion, numismatic coins, and precious metals. He quit his day job, moved a few office supplies into his bedroom, and began his new operation—with less than fifty dollars in cash!

Carl hustled to foster his start-up. He called old suppliers and clients from his former place of business and talked to friends and relatives about his new venture. Slowly he built a clientele and a reputation. But he struggled to grow the business and make ends meet.

After speaking at a trade show in New Orleans, Carl was contacted by one of the people in attendance to discuss investment options. They set up a time to meet a few weeks after the conference. The potential client, a CPA, was interested in investing substantial sums of money but wanted to test the process with Carl's firm using some smaller amounts before engaging in large deals.

The one wrinkle was that the CPA insisted that his transactions be conducted in cash and that nothing be reported to the government. This was soon after the federal government had instituted a new law requiring that all transactions above $10,000 in cash be reported to the IRS. Carl was aware of the new law and explained it to his client. The CPA, however, was adamant: if Carl insisted on reporting the transactions, the CPA would take his business elsewhere.

An intense thirty-minute conversation about compliance with the reporting law occurred. Throughout that exchange Carl pondered his company's precarious financial position and the benefits he would receive from several small investments that would lead to serious money from this demanding client. After a half hour of negotiating, Carl talked himself into doing the deal without reporting anything to the government. As he reflected on the pros and cons of the arrangement, he landed on the side of feeding his family and sustaining his company rather than adhering to the letter of the law. He could not justify passing up the potential profits.

Before finally consenting to move forward, though, the CPA had concerns of his own. Wary of Carl's intentions, he demanded to know how he could be sure that Carl wouldn't mess up the transaction and get them both in trouble. Carl confidently reassured the investor. "There's nothing to worry about. I do this kind of thing all the time. You'll be safe with me." Comforted by Carl's compelling and persuasive manner, the CPA agreed to move ahead with the deal.

After a few transactions were expertly and smoothly handled by Carl, the CPA visited Carl's office with a fellow investor. They slid a briefcase with $200,000 in cash across Carl's desk. Carl had an uneasy feeling about what was going on. This was the payday he had been waiting for, yet he felt queasy inside. After he opened the briefcase to inspect the money, he walked over to his window, which overlooked the building's parking lot. As he pondered the current transaction, he noticed the parking lot was packed with black Crown Victorias. Seconds later there was a loud crash and the door to his office flew off the hinges. Two dozen law enforcement agents rushed into the room, holding badges and guns, while another four dozen held down positions throughout the company office and building. There were agents from the FBI, IRS, Secret Service, and local organized crime units.

It turned out that the CPA wasn't a CPA at all; he was a special undercover agent of the IRS, posing as an investor. Carl was immediately taken into custody, and his company's records were thrown into boxes and hustled into the cars below. The company's employees were shocked.

Eventually Carl was indicted on two counts: illegal racketeering and conspiracy to commit fraud against the federal government. That original thirty-minute conversation, after which Carl decided to knowingly break the law in favor of sustaining his business and family, was going to cost him everything he treasured in this world.

CARL FACES THE MUSIC

As the authorities were preparing their case against Carl, his lawyer discovered that the incriminating tape recording of the initial thirty-minute conversation had somehow been lost. Carl's lawyer was ecstatic and proclaimed that they could beat the charges if Carl would plead not guilty and claim that the conversation never took place. That sent Carl into another round of soul searching.

That's when I entered the picture. As a member of our church in Phoenix, Carl had not only been attending services faithfully for years but also spent a lot of time on the prayer mountain behind our church. Right after he heard the good news from his lawyer about the missing tape, Carl drove to the mountain to seek God's direction. He saw me on the other side of the mountain praying but did not disturb me. But after I returned to my office, he followed me there and asked my assistant if he could get a few minutes alone with me.

"Pastor, I can get out of this mess scot-free if I just tell the judge that the charges against me are false and that I did not do what they claim. But I feel torn as to whether I should be protecting myself or telling the truth. What should I do?"

"Carl," I responded, sensing the pain of indecision and uncertainty that he was enduring, "I know that you'll do the right thing in this situation, because the right thing is always the right thing to do."

I think he was a bit disappointed that I didn't give him a more definitive directive, but he thanked me for my counsel, left my office, and drove directly to the office of the prosecutor. He managed to get past the receptionists and assistants and made his way to the prosecutor's office, where he confronted her. Before she could stop him from talking, he blurted out his confession.

"Ma'am, if you say that what I did is really a crime, then I must be guilty, because I did it." The prosecutor, alarmed by the legal implications of the accused confessing to her, shouted for him to stop talking and to get his lawyer before he said another word. She covered her ears and shooed him out of her office.

Confused by her reaction, Carl left as instructed and called his lawyer, describing what he had just done. A string of profanities coursed through the phone line, along with some impolite questions about Carl's sanity.

The months between his arrest and the trial were the darkest days of Carl's life. He contemplated committing suicide as a way to provide money for his family. He prayed fervently for God's forgiveness. He wallowed in grief, thinking about all the suffering caused by that wrong decision he'd made in a simple half-hour meeting. His business was at a standstill: the company's records had been confiscated, employees had quit out of fear of being tainted by the firm's reputation if there was a fraud conviction, and the office doors had been chained shut. Then word came that the prosecutor was likely to seek a seventeen-year jail sentence for Carl—for acts of dishonesty that he had engaged in and wanted to admit to doing.

After hours and hours of arguments with his own legal team, Carl reached the courtroom on the day of the trial and pleaded guilty to both counts. Before the half-hour sentencing hearing was concluded, the judge asked Carl if he had any final comments. Once again, Carl offered an unexpected comment.

"Your Honor," he said softly, "I don't know why the system is set up the way it is, but if the intention is to scare the daylights out of people like me, and to ensure that we will never break the law again, then I can assure you the system is working. This has been a total nightmare. I am embarrassed by my choices and so sorry for breaking the law. I won't be testing the law in the future."

The judge watched Carl for a few moments and then reviewed a few of the documents in his case file. When at last he responded, the judge miraculously showed Carl grace, giving him five years of probation without any time in prison. "I rarely have guilty people stand before me who not only admit their guilt but also pledge to stay straight," he explained. "Something tells me I should give you a second chance. Don't prove my intuition wrong."

A DESTINY ALTERED

Now, a quarter century later, Carl's life is a dream come true. His business is thriving, having completed billions of dollars of transactions since his day in court. That scary half hour in the courtroom was the beginning of a new life—one in which he strives to always tell the truth and act with integrity. It began when he pleaded guilty, against the advice of his high-powered and well-paid attorneys, simply because it was the truth; and it ended with his admission of remorse and fear in the jaws of the justice system, another unusual expression of honesty and humility.

Against all expectations, Carl describes 1986 as the best year of his life. He now has a healthy marriage to his wife of thirty-five years, a wonderful relationship with his now-grown daughters, and a reputable and profitable company. He is a generous donor to our church and other organizations. He humbly talks about not deserving any of this grace from God, but he loves his life and the opportunities he now has to bless others.

All of this was jeopardized by the power of a half hour. Before the trial, he used that power to bring disgrace and hardship on himself, his family, and his employees. During the trial, he used a half hour to resolve his difficulties by advancing the truth.

How about you? I bet that if you took a half hour right now to make a list of significant choices and actions you've undertaken during the course of your life that happened within a thirty-minute period, or noteworthy outcomes that resulted

from the accumulation of your efforts over a series of related thirty-minute segments, you would be surprised at how much your life has been influenced by
these time blocks.

It's true; you can turn your life—or someone else's—around in thirty minutes. Armed with the Word of God and the ears to hear what God would like to
say to you through His Holy Spirit, things can change radically for the better if
you're willing to invest that little amount of time into getting things right with
God. He won't force you to do so; it's your choice. But it is time well spent.

2

WHY TIME MATTERS

Half-Hour Power Principle:
Small time investments produce huge returns.

We take a lot of things for granted in our lives, such as gravity, air, daylight—and time. Yet time is one of God's most precious gifts to us. It is the most significant nonrenewable resource at our disposal. We have less of it remaining with each passing day. When God gave this gift, He intended for us to use it carefully, intentionally, wisely, and productively.

> Time is the most significant
> nonrenewable resource
> at our disposal.

If your life is a gift from God (and it is!), and time is the organizational foundation of that life, then you are honoring His plan and blessing Him with the fruit of your life when you use your time well. When you serve another person, you are honoring that person with the unique outcome of your irreplaceable existence. Your time is invaluable. You will never get lost time back—and nobody can eliminate the results of time well invested. Wise people will try to use their time for the highest purpose.

I know that how we use time here on earth is important to God. Jesus told us that unless we are faithful in the small things, we will not be entrusted with the greater things of God (see Matthew 25:14–30; Luke 16:10). I assume this means the "little" half hours too.

> Nobody can eliminate the results of time well invested.

Here are a few verses that point this out:

- "Be careful then how you live, not as unwise people but as wise, making the most of the time, because the days are evil. So do not be foolish, but understand what the will of the Lord is" (Ephesians 5:15–17).
- "So teach us to count our days that we may gain a wise heart" (Psalm 90:12).
- "Conduct yourselves wisely toward outsiders, making the most of the time" (Colossians 4:5).
- "LORD, let me know my end, and what is the measure of my days; let me know how fleeting my life is. You have made my days a few handbreadths, and my lifetime is as nothing in your sight. Surely everyone stands as a mere breath" (Psalm 39:4–5).
- "We must work the works of him who sent me while it is day; night is coming when no one can work" (John 9:4).

Time matters!

A HALF HOUR IN HEAVEN

As I've studied the Scriptures now for most of my life, I'm intrigued that to my knowledge the Bible only one time uses a measure of earth time to describe time in heaven. So we talk a lot about eternity in sermons and songs such as "Amazing Grace" ("When we've been here ten thousand years…"), but the Bible itself does not quantify time in heaven—at least like we do now. There is, however, one intriguing exception. Revelation 8:1 says: "When the Lamb opened the seventh seal, there was silence in heaven for about *half an hour*" (emphasis added).

Well, that's pretty interesting—a "half hour" is referred to here. Why?

Honestly, I'm not sure—it remains a mystery. However, I do see two fascinating insights provided in that sentence. First, we are informed that it became silent in heaven. *What?* It had never occurred to me that heaven could be a place without an abundance of sound. The Bible refers our attention to the kinds of noises made in that holy place. In the four chapters in Revelation immediately preceding this passage, we learn that heaven is a place where you'll hear voices like a trumpet blast, the rumble of thunder, constant praise from angels and elders, creatures and choirs singing about the glory of God, the voices of "millions of angels,...living beings and the elders" (5:11, NLT), the sounds of war, the noise of earthquakes, and mighty shouts of worship. That is the normal range of activity inside the gates of the kingdom of God—and it must be noisy!

But there was suddenly silence in heaven. Imagine how startling that must have been.

And notice that this shocking time of quiet lasted for about *thirty minutes.* For the first and only instance on record, the reality of eternity is measured in human time. Nobody knows why that time of silence occurred. But we know that it happened, it was important, and it lasted thirty minutes.

I would like to suggest that the heavenly Father draws our attention to a . thirty-minute span of time because He wants us to understand the significance of small amounts of time, in this case the half hours. If a half hour is important to God, I think it should be important to us as well.

LEARNING THE POWER OF A HALF HOUR

As I began my own ministry career and moved into adulthood, I started to understand more clearly the power of a half hour. I didn't have some single aha moment, but this truth came to me slowly in many circumstances during my formative years—seeds certainly planted in many childhood encounters with my parents, in particular with my dad.

My father was a pastor for decades in Kansas City, Kansas. He was a busy man with a large and demanding church, but he knew how to stop everything and give focused attention. That's the essence of the power of a half hour, by the way: understanding the value of even the smallest increments of time and using those minutes intentionally.

When I was growing up, my dad used to spend time modeling how a leader makes good decisions. He had one of the biggest churches in his denomination and in our region. He had to run a tight ship but was always thoughtful and reasonable in his decisions. What I liked most, though, is that he would stop and take a few minutes to explain to me his thinking and actions in any given situation.

One time my dad was away on a speaking trip and had arranged for a traveling team from the YMCA to do a special presentation at our church. They were a group of young guys who preached the gospel with energy and joy. The local newspaper ran a story about the team the day before they were scheduled to speak. As part of their outreach strategy, the team was presenting a basketball-and-billiards demonstration at the nearby YMCA. I know this seems bizarre these days, but a few of the church's deacons read that story, called an emergency meeting, and then canceled the team's appearance at our church because they were going to *play pool*!

When my dad returned, he was furious and made no effort to hide his anger from the deacons (or anyone else in the church). He and I talked about it at home. I remember him telling me, "What's wrong with playing pool? You hit the ball this way or that way or the other way, and it goes in a pocket. Pool is just a game. The problem is that so often the environment in which that game is played leads to trouble. But pool at the YMCA? What's wrong with that?"

I asked him some questions, and we talked for a while. This process was not unusual. He would put aside his business to spend a half hour teaching me how to think, lead, and make decisions. And then he'd go out and model exactly what we'd talked about.

MEMORABLE HALF HOURS

Life can take dramatic shifts in short periods of time.

When I was beginning my career as a pastor, I dreamed of having a high-powered church in an urban setting. But what actually came available to me was the opportunity to "candidate" at a small church in Davenport, Iowa. When I got a good look at the place—a small, run-down building begging for a bulldozer to end its misery—I was confident there was no way God wanted a "rising star" like me stuck in an unglamorous place like that. But to keep my obligation, I preached both the morning and evening services, but with as little motivation as possible. After the meeting that evening, I was headed out the door, eager to leave Davenport for good, when the church leaders stopped me and asked that I wait until the vote was taken.

What?

The twenty members of the church had gathered for a brief thirty-minute meeting to decide if I was "their man." I almost panicked. *I should have told them there was no way I would accept the job, even if it was offered,* I thought. I waited, and sure enough, with beaming smiles they told me that in a unanimous vote I had been selected. When could I come be their leader?

I pulled out a "God card" and told them I really needed to "pray seriously" before giving them my decision. Actually, what I really wanted to do was buy some time before letting them down easy.

I drove back to Kansas City and wrestled with God for three weeks. *Why had I not told those folks I wasn't interested before their thirty-minute meeting wrecked my life?*

Although I begged God for an opportunity to find a church in LA or New York City, He stamped my passport for Davenport. So I finally gave in and took the job. Of course, God knew what He was doing. Davenport became a place of huge ministry opportunity, and I'll share a few of the great stories from Iowa in this book. The direction of my life, though, was altered by those people casting a vote in a thirty-minute meeting.

Just as your life can change direction in a short time span, you can alter someone else's path in thirty minutes or less.

Some years later, after I had become pastor of a church in Phoenix, a letter came to our church office from a worried mom. She told how her stepson, David, was living in our city and dying of AIDS. He needed hands-on encouragement and love she couldn't provide. He also needed Jesus. One of our visitation volunteers, Fred, took the letter and went looking for David. After several attempts to contact the young man, Fred almost gave up trying to connect. But Fred persisted and finally found David in a local hospital. He was in serious condition and in a quarantine room. After donning protective mask and gloves, Fred made it to David's bedside. After introducing himself and briefly getting acquainted, Fred asked David if he knew Jesus and, if not, did he want to meet Him. David was open and prayed to receive Christ. David was so weak that Fred left after a visit that had lasted only minutes.

> You can alter someone else's
> path in thirty minutes or less.

He returned the next day to find that David was in even worse condition. "Jesus is with you," Fred said.

"He is, He is," David answered weakly. As Fred left, David said weakly, "Thank you."

Fred didn't see David again. He died that night.

THE DARK SIDE OF HALF HOURS

Without much effort you could probably make a pretty long list of ways that you could misspend a half hour. Due to our sinful nature, we can conjure up all sorts of mischief and muster the strength and cleverness to carry out those misdeeds. We have to be careful of the power of a half hour; it can be used for evil as easily as it can be devoted to good.

I have learned this the hard way and once almost lost my life in a half hour.

Some years ago I was on my way to the airport in Los Angeles to catch a flight back to Davenport. I was by myself in my rental car, driving through the crime-ridden neighborhood of Watts—at the time there was no freeway route to LAX. As I made my way through that tough section, a car sped in front of me, cut me off, and then forced me to stop. The driver jumped out and came toward me with a knife. He yelled, "Get out!"

> We have to be careful of the power
> of a half hour; it can be used for evil
> as easily as it can be devoted to good.

I ignored him, backed up my car, and drove off. The guy got in his car, and we both arrived at the next stoplight side by side. Both of us had our windows down. The man wasn't looking at me, but I could see an angry expression on his face. Instead of looking away and maybe saying a prayer for him, I gave in to my own anger and yelled at him, "You're really a big man with that knife, aren't you? How big are you without it?" *Bad move.*

Without saying anything, the guy pulled out a large handgun, pointed it at me, and pulled the trigger. The bullet missed me by about two inches and ended up shattering the back window of my car. This would have been a good time to turn the other cheek, but now I was really mad, so I followed him for several blocks. He stopped at a house and ran indoors. Soon after, he came out and took off again. I finally gave up my chase and called the police.

That was thirty minutes of stupidity. I could have lost my life and surrendered my opportunity to see God do so many wonderful things in my life, including bringing to life our youngest son, Matthew, who had not been born yet.

Even some of the great men in the Bible experienced the tragedy of misused half hours. King David, the man known for his tender heart and courageous behavior, committed his most grievous sins—adultery with Bathsheba and plotting the murder of her husband, Uriah—as the result of watching her bathe and allowing lust to rule his mind and heart. He was not the first—or the last—person to misuse a half hour by contemplating sexual fantasies or conjuring illicit plans related to that lust.

There's definitely a lot of power in a half hour. Good and bad.

THE PRECIOUS GIFT OF TIME

Each day is a gift from God, and I am intentional in how I spend a good deal of my half-hour blocks of time. I deliberately awaken each morning before sunrise to ensure that I am able to start each day with thirty minutes of worship, thirty minutes reading the Scriptures, and thirty minutes of prayer. I prepare my sermons in half-hour blocks of time and find that these bursts of concentration allow me to put forth my best and most focused effort. I schedule counseling appointments as half-hour sessions. When I am writing books, I write thirty minutes at a stretch. Reading books is one of my favorite pastimes; I always have a book with me in case I unexpectedly encounter a half hour of free time during the day. If you need to know where I'll be or what I'll be doing at any time of day, I can pretty much tell you because my day is built on half-hour modules.

> Even in the space of time of a half hour,
> amazing things can happen in your life.

Having said all that, I am not obsessive about my time. God wants us to enjoy life and not feel like every minute has to have some life-altering meaning. Each day should have adequate half hours—many of them unplanned—when you can stop your busyness, interrupt your schedule for an ice-cream cone, play catch with a child, worship the Lord, snuggle with your wife, or encourage a friend—the possibilities are endless. All I want to make you aware of is that even in the space of time of a half hour, amazing things can happen in your life.

What incredible ways will God use the half hours that you will discover in the days ahead? I can't wait to help you find out!

Part 2

The Power of a Half Hour to
CHART YOUR LIFE PATH

3

CLARIFY YOUR VISION AND PURPOSE

Half-Hour Power Principle: Knowing why you are "here" brings deep satisfaction.

I believe each of us is born having some special talent that enables us to do something better than anybody else does. God created every person to do a special thing that He needs done on earth; and if a particular person fails to do that one thing, then it will never be done exactly the way God intended. God will still accomplish His will, but the individual will miss out on the opportunity to play a unique and important role in that activity.

> God created every person to do a special thing that He needs done on earth; and if a particular person fails to do that one thing, then it will never be done exactly the way God intended.

God's unique plans for you relate, of course, to your life vision and purpose. That vision will inspire you, energize you, challenge you, and consume you in the best possible ways. And the only way to get that vision is to spend time humbled in God's presence until He chooses to reveal it to you. That will not happen until He knows that you are devoted to His purposes and can be trusted with the assignment represented by that vision.

> Those who carry out their purpose
> have a chance to do something that
> could change lives for the better.

There is no higher calling you can have than to receive and tirelessly pursue God's unique vision for you. And because God's vision can only be accomplished through the cooperative efforts of people, you will begin to have a sense of how to connect your life with others who will become part of the grand plan for advancing His kingdom.

Those who carry out their purpose have a chance to do something that could change lives for the better. And knowing why you are "here" makes life so much more interesting—and fun!

I can attest to this, since God's vision for my life has long been "to make someone's life better, in the name of Jesus." Because of this I have enjoyed a wonderful life!

Finding Your Purpose

Discovering your life purpose can happen in a half-hour period. These moments of destiny often seem as if they're accidental, as if you just happen to be at a particular place, at a certain time, and prepared for the circumstances. In God's providence, though, those moments and experiences have been provided to prepare you for your destiny to serve God and others.

One of the greatest benefits of periods of focused half hours is that this is often when God implants His vision in your mind and heart. His vision becomes the ultimate dream for your life: a personalized, visualized future that He wants to birth and nurture through you.

After you receive and embrace God's vision for your life, pursue that vision with zeal, conviction, and confidence. The vision will establish your life's purpose and goals.

VISION

It's so critical to understand in what direction God wants you to move. For most of us, indications of that appear when we are young.

What was your childhood and adolescence like? Mine was always a challenge because I was a late bloomer; my growth spurt didn't happen until much later than it did for most of my friends. When you're the peanut in the crowd, people don't take you seriously.

But my size never diminished my dreams of ministry. Watching my father engage in life-changing work as a pastor and leader in the community—he served on the Kansas City Board of Education four terms and ran for mayor of the city—really got me excited. I also hung around with a bunch of kids who were ministry minded.

Things did not get off to a great start for me, though. My best buddy was Bill Baker, a star basketball player. When he announced he was going into ministry, people said, "Praise God. God can use Bill." A week later my classmate Ray Thomas, an outstanding baseball player, announced that he was going into ministry. People rejoiced, saying, "Hallelujah. God will certainly use Ray." Then, a couple of weeks later, I too announced that I wanted to become a pastor. All I heard people say in response to that was "Oh, my God..."

In my late teens, I preached in churches on weekends when a pastor was ill or on a trip. The churches I'd get invited to were usually out in the boondocks— small outposts that had congregations of thirty or forty people. I was grateful for the opportunity to hone my preaching skills and to minister to people, regardless of how many there were. But as time went on, I had an inner conflict. I had a good voice (before I wrecked it by preaching in too many outdoor events and revivals that lacked adequate sound systems) and really wanted to have a gospel singing career, making albums and singing at live events. But I also loved to preach. I was confident enough that I figured maybe I could do it all.

One time during this period of confusion, I flew to Santa Paula, California, to speak at a meeting. I was only about eighteen at the time, and while there I had been asked to record an album at Capitol Records. One of the preachers from Santa Paula drove me down to the recording studio in Los Angeles. On the way we had a conversation about my plans for the future.

I really didn't know what to make of him, but during our thirty-minute conversation about my future he said something that really struck me: "Tommy, you're going to have to decide what you're going to specialize in. What are you going to do? Are you going to preach the Word and pray for people to get healed, or are you going to sing hymns and gospel songs? You've got to be known for one thing that you focus on."

My immediate internal reaction was, *Who are you to be limiting my ministry?* That, obviously, was the arrogance of youth. But the more I thought about his words, the more I realized they were probably true. When push came to shove, it was clear to me that I was called to reach out and win people to the Lord.

That thirty-minute conversation changed my life because it encouraged me to focus on the main thing that God had created me to do.

Are you clear on God's purpose for your life? If not, it's worth spending some specific thirty-minute sessions in prayer asking God to make clear the wonderful path He has designed for you to follow!

4

SOLIDIFY YOUR VALUES

Whatever's really important to you?

It surprises me how so many people have their values defined by external influences, such as their family members or peers, the media, or their experiences. Or there are the internal pressures on values caused by bad thinking or out-of-control feelings. As the Bible says, these folks are "pushed…and butted."[3]

What really matters in life is what's important to God. His values need to be our values.

> What really matters in life
> is what's important to God.

I've heard a number of times that if you take a close look at your checkbook register over a period of a month or two, it will become apparent how you really like to spend your money. That might be one way to identify your values. Or I suppose if we could make a video of your behavior for twenty-four hours of each day during a two-week period, we would start getting a good picture of what drives you.

Yet another way to determine what really motivates you would be to ask that you take a half hour and write down a list of all the things you would like to do in life before you die. This is, of course, what is now called a bucket list—what you want to accomplish before you "kick the bucket"! I actually went through this exercise as a result of a unique encounter.

Reviewing My Values

When I was 20 years old, I took a trip around the world, sharing the gospel in all kinds of places and circumstances. Along the way I'd witnessed remarkable scenes and experienced once-in-a-lifetime thrills. Since then I'd imagined other adventures I could undertake. I didn't seriously consider making any of these adventures a reality—they were simply musings.

Then one day a few years ago, I received a visit from a distinguished gentleman.

An older Jewish man from England made a special trip to visit the Dream Center in Los Angeles. (The Dream Center is part of a ministry to people in need in downtown Los Angeles, led by my son and myself. I'll share more details on this outreach throughout this book.)

This fellow from England had heard about the Dream Center and wanted to personally see how it operated, so he came by the campus and I wound up giving him a tour of the ministry. Before we completed the tour, his eyes were full of tears. He thanked me and then showed up at the church service that night. He put a $25,000 check in the offering and then gave his heart to Jesus when we had the altar call!

After that night he flew all the way from London to Los Angeles every four to six weeks to attend the church services and visit the Dream Center. We discovered that—not surprisingly—he was a very wealthy individual, with successful investments across Europe and the Middle East.

One day he called me to arrange a meeting before the church services that week. When we got together, he was quite excited. "I recently saw a movie that really moved me, called *The Bucket List*," he began. "It caused me to think about my own life and future. Here's what I came up with. Pastor, I want you to create your bucket list—all the things that you've always wanted to do but haven't, and all the places you've always wanted to visit but have not gotten to yet. I've got planes and I've got the money, just like that story. We'll do it. We'll take off several months and just go. What do you say, Pastor? We're not getting any younger. Just you and me, before we get too old, fulfilling our dreams. Come on, let's do it."

That was certainly not the conversation I was expecting. I thanked him and told him I'd get back to him. So I got out my legal pad and asked myself: *What do I want to do? What's really important to me?* I began clicking through the options that came to mind. I didn't want to jump out of an airplane; after all the Bible says "*lo,* I am with you always"[4]—not "*high,* I am with you"! I didn't want to swim with a shark. I had no interest in driving a race car; my wife drives fast enough for me. I've already kissed the most beautiful girl in the world (yes, I mean my wife), and if I were to kiss another she would kill me!

I thought and thought and then thought some more. No matter how hard I tried, I couldn't think of anything I'd rather do than put food in another hungry belly or give another altar call or have more opportunities to serve people.

It turns out that my life's everyday activity *was* my bucket list. It goes along with the prayer I've recited for years: *Lord, when I get too old to do what I'm doing, just let me die. What is there to live for but serving your people?*

That surprising visit with the man from England forced me to spend time reflecting on the life the Lord has given me and to realize I'm clear on my values. When I settled down to think clearly about what was really important to me or what I might like to do, I realized that my bucket list really had only one item: I love serving hurting people.

That half hour of reflection helped remind me what ultimately motivates me and makes me tick.

If you needed to make a list, what key values would you record?

5

SHARPEN YOUR GIFTS AND ABILITIES

Half-Hour Power Principle:
Use the tools from your God-given kit.

God has blessed you with a variety of gifts and abilities. Those talents become more strategic and influential—for your benefit and assistance to others—when you invest in developing and sharpening them. And it's amazing how much sharpening can occur in thirty-minute blocks of time.

Various passages of the Bible discuss the fact that God gives spiritual gifts to those whom He calls to His service. Because the ways we can serve the Lord are so diverse—from being a loving husband and parent, to helping kids learn while teaching in a public school, to praying for discouraged friends, to donating money to the less fortunate, to more formal types of ministry in a church setting—each of us receives a different mix of gifts. But they are all provided to us for the same purpose: to bless others for the glory of God.

If you love Jesus as your Lord and Savior, you have gifts from the Holy Spirit at your disposal. You might think of those gifts as supercharged abilities. But just as a baseball player has an unusual talent for hitting or pitching the ball, that talent has to be developed. Spiritual gifts are the same: you must cultivate spiritual gifts through study, practice, and application.

What happens when you commit yourself to maturing your gifts? You become capable of accomplishing superior outcomes.

> You must cultivate spiritual gifts through study, practice, and application.

The Bible tells us about all kinds of individuals—who were no different from you or me—who took their gifts seriously and worked at refining them until they were unusually capable.[5]

- Samuel became a great prophet by working with Eli to understand and expand his gift.
- As a shepherd David perfected the use of a slingshot, which came in handy in his battle against Goliath.
- Apollos was a gifted speaker with a good heart, but it took mentoring from Aquila and Priscilla to enhance his abilities as an evangelist and apologist.
- Peter was given a master's course in leadership, which helped convert him from an impetuous bungler into a reasoned and seasoned elder.
- Even Paul transitioned from being an angry scholar to a loving teacher beyond compare.

God has similar plans to use the gifts He's placed in you and me.

MAKING THE MOST OF SKILLS

A great example of someone who has made the most of the abilities God gave him is a man named Bill Wilson. I first met him many years ago during a speaking engagement in St. Petersburg, Florida. Bill was a young guy who I noticed was following me everywhere I went, watching everything I did. It kind of freaked me out! Bill was really skinny and had long hair—I wasn't sure what to make of him.

Finally we had a chance to get acquainted, and I found out he was aware of our church in Iowa and what we did to reach people. He told me he had a school bus that had been donated for use at his church's vacation Bible school, but he didn't know what to do with the bus the rest of the year.

Our church in Davenport was one of the pioneers of large-scale bus ministry, so I sat down with Bill and gave him a personal thirty-minute clinic on how to do bus outreach. I described how to get a bus pastor, ways of recruiting kids, the kind of drivers to recruit, how to keep kids coming back every week, how to address the concerns and questions of the kids' parents, and so forth.

Bill really got into it. He was a great children's pastor, and he truly grasped the value of the bus ministry. The next thing I knew, he had ten buses running at his church. Then one day he called and talked about coming to work for me as a children's pastor and leader of our bus ministry. We talked for a half hour, and then I hired him. Not long after he started with us, he had forty-seven buses running! After a while, about the same time I decided to go from pastoring in Iowa to a small church in Phoenix, he met with me again and said, "Pastor, I know you've always wanted to reach New York City, so I'm going to go there, and you can live vicariously through me."

So I moved to Phoenix, and Bill started what eventually became the famous Metro Ministries (now known as Metro World Child) for children in New York City. It is a model that is now used all over the world.

I attribute Bill's success in ministry to a series of thirty-minute encounters we had over the years, starting with that half hour in Florida and then the half-hour job interview that led him to develop the concept and then launch one of the most successful children's ministries in history. Bill was willing to pay the price of cultivating his vision and skills to fulfill his purpose in life.

THIRTY MINUTES TO FINE-TUNE YOUR GIFTS

Imagine what would happen if you devoted a half hour every day—or even just once a week—to honing the spiritual gifts that God has entrusted to you. Because your gifts are provided specifically to help you fulfill your God-given purpose in life, you would be better equipped, more efficient, and undeniably successful thanks to your commitment to growing your gifts.

Over the course of my lifetime, I have been blessed to expand my ministry tool kit. Music is a passion of mine, and even though I'm not much of a musician, I learned how to play the piano by working at it for thirty minutes a day, day after day, week after week, when I was young. Nobody will ever confuse me with Vladimir Horowitz or Van Cliburn, but my skills have assisted in ministry efforts many times.

> Imagine what would happen if you devoted a half hour every day—or even just once a week—to honing the spiritual gifts that God has entrusted to you.

My counseling skills went from nonexistent to viable, thanks to my determination to be the best counselor I could be, knowing that it is one of the chief ways that a pastor is able to serve God's people.

One of the best ways to grow your skills, gifts, talents, and abilities is to observe others who possess similar capacities and imitate their best practices. For instance, one of the men who literally changed my life was Billy Graham. He was in Oakland one time while I happened to be there. I showed up, along with many others, to hear him speak in a busy public square the day before his crusade began in San Francisco. I carefully watched him as the rally unfolded outdoors at lunchtime. He stirred my creativity and led me to believe that every Sunday at church could be as exciting as a mini Billy Graham crusade. From that experience I realized I could spend each week motivating everyone in each of our ministries (275 of them) to be passionate about bringing hurting and unsaved people to church. And then every Sunday morning could be like the Super Bowl or mini Billy Graham crusade—an exciting, high-quality time of ministry.

Watching that half-hour lunchtime event in Oakland put an unquenchable dream in my heart that the Lord has allowed us to bring to pass—on a smaller scale than a Super Bowl but a memorable experience for those who participate.

Part 3

The Power of a Half Hour to

STRENGTHEN
YOUR FAITH

MAKE A REGULAR CONNECTION

Half-Hour Power Principle:
Pursue the best relationship imaginable.

I do not know God's specific vision for your life—that's unique and between the two of you. But I do know that His desire is for you to love Him with all your heart, soul, mind, and strength. That's a mission that all Christ-followers have in common. Knowing and persistently pursuing that goal will give us direction and fulfillment that we would not otherwise experience.

So how do we grow in loving God with all we possess? The most important element of your faith is the relationship you develop with God and how you maintain that relationship. The Bible says that when we draw near to Him, He will draw near to us.[6] I know from many years of experience that a consistent investment of half hours creates an environment conducive to getting closer to God and maturing my faith.

Many people think that being a genuine follower of Christ is too hard. They resist the effort because they say they could never be perfect—which is true—but then God never asked you to be perfect, only to be repentant and willing to let Jesus do the heavy lifting for you.

Other people abandon God because they think they've done such bad stuff in their lives that He would never accept them. That's not true either. That's the reason Jesus died on the cross: to forgive sinners like you and me of all the rotten things we've done that offend Him.

Others seem to think that if they go to church regularly, think highly of Jesus, and call themselves Christians, then they have done all they need to do. Tragically, that describes tens of millions of people in America, but that view is wrong as well. God is after a growing relationship, not an empty routine; He wants to be the center of your life, not to simply be imbedded in a slice of it.

As you reflect on what it takes to have a deep and ever-growing relationship with Him, realize that just as in any other significant relationship, you can make the foundations stronger and deeper by regularly investing a little time to build that connection.

> God wants to be the center of your life,
> not to simply be imbedded in a slice of it.

Thirty minutes alone with God will change your life. Do it regularly, and you will be a new person. God will never waste your time! Even if you are merely quiet and still in His presence, you will emerge a changed person. The beauty of such a commitment is that any time you have a free half hour is time you can use to pursue an intimate connection with God.

MY SPIRITUAL ROUTINE

Years ago I began a daily spiritual routine that has helped me tremendously. What has been most helpful about the routine is that the elements occur in thirty-minute bursts and that structure is unchanging. But the experiences within the structure are new each day. Let me explain.

Long ago I made a commitment to the Lord that the first person I would talk to in the morning—even before my wife—would be God. That may sound corny, but it reflects my devotion to humble myself before God and to recognize that He is my most important relationship and that I take my marching orders for the day and throughout the day from Him. He's in charge, and I am happy to serve Him as He chooses.

One of the unexpected benefits of this practice is that by spending my first half hour of the day in God's presence, thanking and praising Him, it helps me get locked in with Him for the rest of the day. If you spend thirty minutes being intimate with someone, it changes you for the rest of your day. When that intimacy has been shared with God, you're definitely getting your day off on the right foot.

Immediately after my worship time with Him, I spend a second thirty minutes reading the Bible. To appreciate the importance of this activity, you need to realize how much I look forward to reading the newspaper when I wake up! I want to know what's going on out there, and I believe that it's easier to impact the world if I know what's happening in it. But a firm rule of mine is that before I read the newspaper, I want to put my mind into the Word of God to get my thinking headed in the right direction.

My daily time reading the Scriptures in the morning is not just a shallow tradition that I mindlessly follow. The Bible is truly a sacred book and a treasured gift to me from God. Before I start to read it each morning, I remind myself that if Jesus came back and preached at my church, He would preach from this very same book that He has given me. I marvel that I hold in my hand the eternal Word of God, His actual words and perfect revelation. He would not add to it nor take away from it if He were here today.

Being privileged enough to have the words of God in my hands, I must not treat the Bible flippantly. Through that book I will hear from God as if He were here and speaking audibly to me. To make the most of the reading experience, I have to prepare my heart to enter His presence and absorb His words.

In just thirty minutes God can revolutionize your thinking, if you let Him. And the more consistently you spend time and thought addressing His words to you, the deeper understanding you'll achieve and the greater your love for Him and His Word will be.

I am not saying you should imitate my routine; I am suggesting you develop a routine that works for you. But don't ignore the importance of developing personal spiritual habits. It doesn't take much time. We often get caught up in the busyness of each day, and before you know it, God has slipped a few notches down our priority list. If you establish habits that put God in first place, and that keep Him there, you'll be better off because of them.

7

FRIENDS "HANG OUT"

Half-Hour Power Principle:
Be honest and transparent with your best Friend.

I treat prayer as if I am spending time with my best friend.

What do you do when you're with your best friend? You do pretty much whatever you feel like doing, right? It's your chance to get comfortable and be yourself. That translates into each day's conversation with God being different. I try to always be open and real when I'm in God's presence. He is my best Friend, and that's how I am with my best earthly friends too.

> Always be open and real
> when in God's presence.

Many people develop a personal prayer regimen. Mine is a bit unusual. Every day, besides praying during my first thirty minutes after waking up, I spend another thirty minutes later going to the mountain behind our church. I climb to the top of that mountain and sit on one of the flat rocks that overlooks the city. Remember, we live in Phoenix, so it's hot up there, but I rarely notice the heat because I'm so immersed in my conversation with God. I have literally worn a path about a foot deep up there where I walk around and praise the Lord, thanking Him for His blessings.

When I go to the mountain to pray, I always take a few moments to prepare. I start by reminding myself that in a very focused way I am about to enter the holy presence of the King of kings—the Creator of the universe and the One who is the Judge of my soul and Lover of my being. I know that if I were going to visit the queen of England or meet the president, I'd take the time to learn the proper protocol before entering their presence. And here I am, climbing the mountain to speak to the King of kings and Lord of lords, so I must prepare my heart, mind, and soul, not taking this privilege for granted but recognizing that this is a special moment, a holy time, a significant event in my life.

Once I arrive at the top of the mountain, I start by praising God and then open my prayer by saying, "Holy Spirit, You're my prayer partner. And before I go to the Lord, I'm going to run my prayer requests by You," because the Holy Spirit acts as a kind of translator for my words to God and will filter out the dumb requests that I'm inclined to make. I may pray, "Holy Spirit, You know I need a new car. I really like that Rolls Royce." The Holy Spirit will reply, "Well, that's nice, but that SUV's good enough for you." Or I'll say, "Holy Spirit, I speak to thousands of people representing God. I need that $3,000 designer suit." And the Holy Spirit will respond, "I agree; you need a new suit. That black one at the mall is just right for you."

Then I take the Holy Spirit with me to the Father. After I spend time praising Him and maybe presenting a few requests, it's not uncommon for me to run out of things to say. That's when my prayer partner, the Holy Spirit, takes over on my behalf, praying with deep groanings I do not know or understand and telling God what I really need.[7] As a result, the Lord has given me things that I never even asked for; He has provided me with things that bring me joy that I didn't even know would bring me joy.

Some days I have a lot I want to say to God, and I pretty much chatter at Him the whole time. Other days I cannot help but spend most of the time rejoicing and praising Him. Sometimes I go up the mountain and just weep. Occasionally I get to the top and just sit there and say, "Lord, I don't feel like talking. You just talk to me." Those are the times I hear most clearly from Him.

Once I got in the habit of spending thirty minutes on the mountain seeking

God, my whole life changed. My relationship with God was transformed, as was my understanding and experience of the Holy Spirit. The Holy Spirit has become a friend and a prayer partner—one who has completely altered my life.

After this half-hour conversation with the Lord, when I come down from the mountain, I am always a different person. I don't care how big a problem I am wrestling with, by the time I reach the bottom of the mountain I usually either have come up with a solution or at least have a better sense of how to cope with the matter. My time praying on the mountain every day isn't just a way of allowing God to break through with solutions to my issues; it is a time when I receive a sense of peace in my heart from spending time with God and sensing Him at work in my life.

There are many ways to connect with God—He is such a creative and available listener and friend! But I highly recommend that you take advantage of some private, daily, thirty-minute visits with Him.

8

LISTEN

Half-Hour Power Principle:
When visiting with God,
don't do all the talking.

One of the keys to successful connection times with God is the ability to listen for His guidance. To some people that might sound spooky or just plain crazy. But the truth is that God speaks to His people. He doesn't speak to everyone in the same way, and He certainly doesn't speak to us on command. But no matter how He chooses to speak to you, you can be quite certain that you won't hear Him at all if you're always talking and busy.

When God speaks, He tends to tailor the message to who you are and the method to the means that will communicate with you most effectively. Some people literally hear a voice that they believe is His way of talking to them. Others see visions that provide direction or correction. A common experience is for God to speak to people directly through the Bible, where a particular passage strikes the reader as God's special and direct revelation at that moment. Often God will speak to a believer through the words of another believer, using that person as a messenger to convey God's plan.

God's primary way of connecting with me is through impressions. When I pray about something and wait for Him to respond, I will often receive a sense or impression of what should be done or how to proceed in a given situation. Naturally, I cannot receive that impression if I'm too busy telling God things He already knows.

So it takes more than just being silent and still; you also have to be receptive to whatever message God wants to deliver to you while you're accessible. It's like the great football coach Lou Holtz said: "I never learned anything…by talking. The only times I've ever learned anything were by listening or reading."[8]

> Waiting on the Lord is not
> just sitting in silence,
> killing time.

Some people think of quiet time as wasted time. I think part of the reason is that they misunderstand how to use that time of stillness. They look at thirty minutes of waiting on the Lord as a half hour that could have produced something. But if you use that period of time wisely, you do produce something that's invaluable: readiness.

Waiting on the Lord is not just sitting in silence, killing time. It is your moment to get in sync with the mind and heart of God in anticipation of getting His marching orders and the signal to get going. It's like someone who competes in track. The runner gets his feet positioned and then gets his body ready to take off at the gunshot. He is waiting for the right moment to take off, but he's preparing himself before that moment. Waiting on the Lord is not about retreating into comfort; it's about receiving the insights and wisdom you need to fulfill the tasks God has given you. Like that runner, the key is listening to the instructions you receive. For the runner, they are "on your mark," "get ready," and then *bang*! Off you go.

For the person who is still before the Lord, there will be perfect instructions for his or her situation. If you listen and follow those instructions, success will follow. Sometimes it may take time before you're given the "go" command, but there is always a good reason.

BEING STILL DURING DRIVE TIME

Of course you don't need to be sequestered in a quiet room by yourself or on top of a mountain praying to reap the benefits of being quiet and still before God. A person in our church, J. J. Hayes, discovered a helpful practice during her days working at a large Phoenix corporation. Here's her story.

When I moved to Phoenix, my apartment turned out to be located pretty far from my first job, so my commute was about thirty minutes each way. One day I decided to turn everything off on purpose during my drive to work. You know how it is: once you wake up, you quickly turn on something that makes noise; there's always noise. I thought I'd try driving without the noise. And Pastor Barnett had said something in a message about noise, how we always have to have noise. And so I said, "Okay, for these thirty minutes that I'm driving, I'm going to purposely have no noise."

So I turned everything off—my sports radio, my worship CDs— and I decided to make my commute that morning a purposeful, quiet half hour. So while I was driving that familiar route, I began kind of talking to God. A lot of the ride was totally quiet, and it was amazing to me that after that half hour, by the time I pulled into the parking lot at work, I realized the need for more changes in my life than I had ever recognized before. It dawned on me that we get so busy and distracted that it's not until we stop some of our normal activities that we really actually realize what needs to change and how to make those changes. And I'm not talking about minor changes, like how I'm combing my hair. It was a great time for me to notice some major flaws in my character and in my personality.

Well, after that experience I decided that from then on I would use my drive time to be quiet before God and try really hard to hear what He had to tell me. That drive helped me realize that for me to see the changes necessary in my life or even in a given situation, I have to stop, be still, and be quiet. I'm a product of my society, so I'm very much a doer, so to break away from that routine and stop it has to be a definite commitment, something I do on purpose.

At first it was really hard to maintain that practice. I was really uncomfortable with the silence; I was used to noise all around me all the time. The quiet made me realize I'm actually alone. And I'll never forget the first few times I almost turned the radio on, just to have some noise. It was really hard, but the more I got used to it, I even began to look forward to it. After a while I even did it on the way home from work too. I started to really enjoy that time because it became time with God and a period of stillness, and I felt peaceful when I got out of my car. It gave me time to process everything and to enjoy the power in stillness. For me, that driving was time that I grew.

After I left that job and took one closer to my home—I know this sounds funny or weird—sometimes I still will get in my car and drive around a while so I have that time of stillness. I can't do it at home for some reason, at least not yet, so this has become a valuable part of my life.

J. J. enthusiastically endorses the concept of being still before God—even if you're moving at seventy miles per hour!

You never know when a half hour of quietness might present itself to you. Will you choose to fill it with noise and other distractions, or will you use that time to let God break through the cacophony of your life and touch your heart?

Part 4

The Power of a Half Hour to
BUILD YOUR CHARACTER

9

HUMBLE YOURSELF

Half-Hour Power Principle:
Go "low" so God can lift you "high."

The Bible highlights the importance of having a humble attitude. Such humility is built on the foundation that you are indeed special, dearly loved by God, and created to accomplish His unique plan for you.

Some of the superstars of the Bible weighed in on the importance of humility. Solomon, the wisest of the wise, noted that pride brings a person down while humility precedes being honored by others. Jesus told His followers that those who exalt themselves are in for a surprise because they will be humbled in spite of their inflated sense of self-worth. Peter exhorted the early Christians, and us, through his writing, to be clothed with humility.[9]

What can we do in thirty-minute blocks to make us more humble people? A tremendous amount!

Leaders, in particular, often struggle with humility. Yet when a leader incorporates authentic humility into his or her attitude, it is compelling. A great example of the matter-of-fact nature of true humility was recently demonstrated by Peter Chiarelli, a four-star general in the US Army and the second-highest ranked officer in that branch. General Chiarelli was attending a special dinner event at the White House. He was walking across the room, en route to his seat, when he passed behind one of the president's advisors, who was already seated at her table and engaged in conversation. With a quick sideways glance behind herself, she saw the stripe down the general's pants and assumed it was one of the waiters. Without looking up or disengaging from her conversation, she requested another glass of wine from the passing "waiter." The general, amused by the misunderstanding, made his way over to a serving station, picked up a bottle of wine, returned to the table, and poured the beverage in her glass.

When the president's advisor finally looked up to thank the supposed waiter, she realized her mistake and a horror-struck look overcame her face. She began to stand to offer her apology, but the general laughed off the incident and wished her a pleasant evening.[10]

That kind of grace charms people. But it's not always as easy as the general made it seem. A friend who is a successful author, having written dozens of best-selling books, confided to me that criticism of his manuscripts by editors used to rub him the wrong way.

"I'd look at the inane comments they plastered all over my work and ask myself, *Who do these people think they are? What have they ever written that the public embraced? How many bestsellers had they written?* I thought of editors as wannabe writers who got their enjoyment from ripping apart the work of 'real writers.'

"Rather than letting this process anger me with each submission, I flew to the publishing house to have a face-to-face meeting with the latest editor that had been assigned to me. I planned to spend a half hour telling her off and putting her in her place so she wouldn't be a nuisance to me during my next project.

"Fortunately, she was a very humble, compassionate lady whose love of good composition and intelligent writing was unmistakable. The more we talked, the more excited I became about the contribution she could make to help me become a better writer. Her expertise and passion pretty much shamed me into humility. That half-hour meeting led to weekly phone conversations about writing that have boosted me to the next level of quality."

Humility Helps

You hear a lot of talk about having an attitude of humility, but you don't see it as often as you might expect. Here are a few things I've observed over the years that can help you develop that spirit of humility—and these are all things that you can practice every day in a half hour or less.

- Come up with a series of phrases or responses you can use in different situations to indicate that you are nothing special or that your action deserves no special recognition. Uttering phrases like "it was my pleasure" after being thanked, or "I'd be happy to help you with that" are examples of this kind of self-effacing, other-person-first kind of thinking.

- Develop ways you can compliment or give credit to others who have worked with you on projects. This comes off as phony unless you can truly muster an appreciation for the contributions or abilities of those with whom you have worked. Taking the time to identify and then communicate the positive effort, skills, and ideas that people have provided will probably change your attitude about yourself as well as those whom you are praising.

- Get together with coworkers, friends, and family members with the sole intention of listening to what's on their minds. If you can do this without the expectation of taking over the conversation or topping their miseries with a litany of your own, you will encourage them. Placing the focus on others will convey the worth you assign to them in your mind and heart.

- Contact someone with whom you have had a disagreement and admit that you were wrong. When you sincerely acknowledge your error or apologize for something you did that was wrong or inappropriate, it tells the individual that you are an honest, well-intentioned person committed to truth and relationship—that it's more important to you to be connected than right.

- Go out of your way to thank others who have helped you grow. They have added value to your life; acknowledge their input and the positive influence it has had on who you are and what you are capable of producing. The fact that you are recognizing their superiority as the teachers and your status as the student reflects a humble and grateful spirit. In the same vein, look for someone who desires growth in an area of expertise you possess, and then offer to mentor him or her.

- Embrace someone else's idea that competes with one that you have offered. Indicate clearly that you feel his or her idea is a better concept and will be more useful than your suggestion. Give that idea your full support as you move toward a solution or final product, accepting it as if it were your own but without trying to take any credit for it.

These are just a few ways to practice humility in short periods of time.

GROWING IN HUMILITY

My parents got married during the Great Depression, a few years before the outbreak of World War II. They were a study in contrasts: my mother was very shy, while my dad was an outgoing pastor/evangelist. My father's evangelistic ministry took him all over the country for revival meetings, as he preached in cities as well as small towns.

In the early years of their marriage, before they had children, my mother traveled with my dad to many of those events. To help out, she was a soloist. She really wasn't a great singer, but she was trying her best to support her husband and be a blessing to him and those who attended.

Invitations to future revival meetings came from pastors who were attending to check out the evangelist and judge whether or not he would be effective in their communities. One night a couple of pastors came to see my father preach at a tent meeting in Texas. Travel was quite different back then; there weren't motels and hotels readily available or affordable, so it was a common practice for visiting pastors to stay in the homes of local pastors or at church facilities. At this particular revival, my parents happened to be staying in the same parsonage as the two pastors who had come to evaluate my father's preaching. After the service ended, my mother returned to the parsonage, while my dad stayed behind to minister to people. It was a hot and humid Texas night, and, of course, there was no air conditioning in those days. Everyone had their windows open, hoping for a breeze to cool things down.

My mom lay down on her bed to go to sleep, and because the windows were open, she heard the visiting pastors talking to each other in their bedroom. One of them remarked how much he liked my father's preaching, saying he thought the young pastor would go far and have a successful national ministry. The other pastor agreed with him but added a caveat: "But he does have one serious handicap. That wife of his…she's so shy and backward. Mark my words, she'll be a stumbling block to him. She could hold him back from being successful."

Ouch! As my mother lay in that hot bedroom and heard those words, tears of sadness rolled down her cheeks. After she silently shut the window, she returned to the bed and softly spoke a prayer, "God, I am not going to be a stumbling block. I am going to make something of myself. With Your help, I will be a blessing to him."

True humility involves making an honest assessment of yourself—determining the *truth*. My mom's feelings were hurt, but she also knew there was some truth to the criticism—and that there were things she could do to improve herself.

> True humility involves making an honest assessment of yourself—determining the truth.

God answered her prayer. Sure enough, she became a great counselor. There were numerous occasions when people would fly in from different parts of the world to seek her counsel. She developed expertise in handwriting analysis, which brought her international recognition and opportunities. She also directed all the pageants that were held by my dad's church—pageants that were a big part of his outreach ministry. Anyone who knew her later in life would be shocked to discover her shaky start. My dad would be the first to sing her praises and admit that she was a very significant partner in his ministry. But it all sprang from that conversation she overheard and the subsequent half hour of self-examination that motivated her to seek a more fruitful ministry, based on blessing my father so that he could bless others.

An old saying reminds us that there are two types of people in this world: those who come into a room and say, "Well, here I am!" and those who come in and say, "Aha, there you are." Which type are you? Take a close look at your attitude, and then see if humility is one of your stronger character traits.

10

REPENT AND FORGIVE

Half-Hour Power Principle:
Forgiveness brings freedom.

In a competitive, fast-paced, materialistic world like ours, it's easy to develop and hold on to grudges or to seek personal gain at the expense of others. This attitude of selfishness simply brings division and ugliness to the world. A more fruitful attitude is one in which we quickly and willingly repent of the errors we commit, and just as quickly and willingly forgive those who seek our forgiveness.

I encourage you to regularly take a half hour and ask the Lord to make you aware of any people whom you need to forgive. Then take the additional half hours needed to actually contact the people and ask for forgiveness. This is a serious matter to God, as was revealed when Jesus said, "If you forgive those who sin against you, your heavenly Father will forgive you. But if you refuse to forgive others, your Father will not forgive your sins" (Matthew 6:14–15, NLT).

> Ask the Lord to make you aware of any
> people whom you need to forgive.

I recall one situation in which I needed to be both repentant and forgiving. It happened in reaction to a letter from a woman who visited our church. She had seen me on a television show and visited because she thought I would be the

loving pastor she was searching for. As her letter made abundantly clear, I was
not what she expected.

> I came to your church last Sunday morning. I couldn't get out of
> there fast enough after the service was over. The singing was too
> fast. Your preaching was too fast. On the way out I saw all those
> wheelchairs in the front of the auditorium and went up there. I
> tried to help one of the ladies push the wheelchair out, but she
> wouldn't let me. My morning at your church was an awful experi-
> ence. I will not be returning.

Naturally, I did not have a chance to explain that the reason the wheelchair
assistants would not allow her to help was because of the insurance regulations
we must abide by in order to be covered. The assistants are specially trained to
handle the wheelchairs; they know how to put them on the bus lifts and secure
them in place. We have ten buses designed solely to hold wheelchairs, and we
fill those buses every weekend. What she interpreted as cruelty was people doing
their job by the rules.

I'm human, so my natural tendency was to want to send her a scathing letter
in response. But I thought about it for a couple of days, and then I sat down and
wrote her an apology.

> *Dear So-and-So,*
>
> *I'm so sorry that I disappointed you on your visit to our church. I
> apologize that you were let down by the message and the music.
> To be honest with you, I don't like my preaching half the time.
> Sometimes I think to myself that I ought to resign and let a
> younger, more qualified man come that would do a better job.
> I'd appreciate it if you would pray for me because I too get
> discouraged about my preaching.*

*As for the music, our choir and instrumentalists are volunteers,
and I think they do a wonderful job of helping us to worship
God. But I know the music doesn't please everybody. It is hard to
find just the right mix that will satisfy young people, parents, and
seniors. We do our best, but obviously we do not satisfy everyone's
expectations.*

*Finding a great church can be a difficult task sometimes. I am
grateful that you gave us a try. I hope that you will forgive me and
our church for our failings. I hate to disappoint people who are
seeking God; it absolutely breaks my heart. I love you and wish you
the best in your search for a great church home.*

Then I went down to our church bookstore and bought a really expensive
Bible, had her name embossed on it, and enclosed a handwritten card that said,
"Please accept this as a token of my love and regret." We sent it off to her, and I
expected that to be the end of the story.

The next Wednesday night after the close of our service, I was meeting with
people afterward. There was a small line of people waiting to see me. One of
them was a well-groomed, sophisticated-looking lady whom I did not recognize.
When her turn came for us to speak, she burst into tears. "I'm the woman. I'm
the woman," she said. Those are words no guy ever likes to hear, but since I've
been faithful to my wife my whole life, I was puzzled.

"What woman?" I asked.

Between sobs she blurted out, "I'm the woman that wrote you that letter." I
still did not understand what she meant until I noticed the Bible clutched in her
hands, held against her chest. It was the embossed Bible I had sent. Perhaps she
saw me staring at the Bible because then she said, "And this is the dearest thing
to me."

She tried unsuccessfully to end her crying but continued her explanation.
"Your preaching was wonderful. This service was wonderful. My husband beat
me before I came to church tonight. He forbids me to attend church, he's mean

to me, and I'm a bitter woman." I gave her a big hug and told her I loved her. Soon thereafter she got saved and became a member of our church. To God's glory, her husband later came and also accepted Christ.

The lesson for me was the importance of responding in love, not anger, and waiting for the Lord to direct my response. What a difference it made in three lives.

This is the beauty of genuine repentance and forgiveness. I know of nothing else that has the potential to make your life more satisfying! Jesus will carry your burdens. Your role is to surrender the agony of holding on to unrepented sin and retained bitterness toward others.

Set yourself free!

11

OWN A GREAT ATTITUDE

Half-Hour Power Principle:
Shift your outlook to change your destiny.

One of America's great Olympic athletes is Scott Hamilton. He was a four-time world skating champion, four-time US champion, and Olympic gold medalist. He is also well known for his tireless support of the underprivileged, working with the Special Olympics, Make-A-Wish Foundation, and a variety of medical research centers.

Scott has survived three operations related to brain tumors but has never lost his giving spirit. People are drawn to Scott because of his upbeat, humorous, sincere, and friendly attitude. One of his great sayings comes directly out of his personal experience: "The only disability in life is a bad attitude."[11]

Let's face it: for a variety of reasons, each of us can fall into a funk in our thought life. I'm amazed how helpful it can be to take just thirty minutes to reflect on how that negative attitude can get readjusted.

> "The only disability in life is a bad attitude."
> —Scott Hamilton

I've often pondered the fact that if I have been made in the likeness of God, and He visited Earth to give humans a demonstration of what godliness is like, then I should imitate His attitude as best I can. What words would you choose to describe Jesus's attitude? Some that have come to my mind include *confident, determined, loving, compassionate,* and *creative.* Although many people act as if their attitude is determined by others, you alone are responsible for it.

> "We have a choice every day regarding the attitude we will embrace for that day."
> —Chuck Swindoll

One of America's renowned teaching pastors, Chuck Swindoll, has spoken frequently about the importance of your attitude in life. Here is a sample of what he has to say on the subject:

> Attitude, to me, is more important than facts. It is more important than the past, than education, than money, than circumstances, than failures, than successes, than what other people think or say or do. It is more important than appearance, giftedness, or skill. It will make or break a company, a church, or a home. The remarkable thing is we have a choice every day regarding the attitude we will embrace for that day. We cannot change our past. Nor can we change the fact that people will act in a certain way. We also cannot change the inevitable. The only thing that we can do is play on the one string we have, and that is our attitude. I am convinced that life is 10 percent what happens to me and 90 percent how I react to it. And so it is with you—we are in charge of our attitudes.[12]

Your attitude is so much more than whether you are positive or negative toward the world around you. Your attitude is a central part of who you are—and many people define you according to the attitude you project.

Every hour of every day you are making choices about the attitude you adopt. The attitude you embrace is a decision you make. And the great thing is that an attitude can be changed quickly. But sometimes we need to stop for a half hour and do an attitude adjustment.

Social scientists have discovered that we often assume the same attitude over and over—in other words, it is a habit we have developed. But that also means that your attitude is under your control, and, therefore, you can reshape it in some pretty astonishing and beneficial ways—if you take full advantage of the thirty-minute opportunities that arise throughout your day.

Sports are a great example of the importance of attitude. Countless coaches have observed that if their team believes they will lose, they will certainly lose; but if the team believes in itself, it has a chance to win. Think about how fortunes change at halftime—that twenty- to thirty-minute period of time to re-adjust to reality. Great coaches are able to sense when their teams are suffering from self-doubt, fear, or complacency. Those are the coaches who motivate the team to change their attitude into a winning mind-set. Strategy and talent are important, but if a talented team following a great game plan doesn't believe in itself—or the strategy—it is very likely to lose.

There is nothing more exciting than watching a team that was lethargic or disengaged in the first half come roaring out of the locker room to play up to its potential in the second half. Dig deep enough and you frequently discover it was because of a shift in attitude that was initiated at the half.

Thirty Minutes to a Better Attitude

There are numerous attitudes we could discuss, but do you see how you can use a mere thirty minutes to facilitate a serious attitude adjustment? At the end of the day people are more likely to remember you for your attitude than for your appearance, intelligence, or talent. If nothing else, remember that a positive attitude may not solve all your problems, but it will annoy enough people who don't have one to make it worth the effort! You can be happy or sad, confident or fearful, optimistic or pessimistic, loving or hateful, selfish or other centered. The choice is yours; the amount of work is the same, whichever attitude you choose.

12

PRACTICE "GR-ATTITUDE"

Half-Hour Power Principle:
Make being thankful a habit.

Investing thirty minutes every day toward expressing gratitude changes your outlook on life for the rest of the day—and beyond.

Many people don't think about the subconscious habits that produce their attitudes: habits of thinking, habits of behavior, and habits of belief. This did not dawn on me until I began to cultivate the habit of spending a half hour each day being intentionally grateful for specific people in my life, the opportunities I have, experiences and possessions I can enjoy, and the skills and abilities that allow me to be a productive individual.

There are different ways of engaging in this practice. For instance, almost every morning I spend thirty minutes writing thank-you notes at the bottom of the receipts to be sent to people who have donated money to the Dream Center. I guess it's old-fashioned to have a P.S. at the end of the letter—these days it's kind of old-fashioned to send a letter!—but then I always add a handwritten note and add my initials. It's a lot of work and takes some creativity to avoid falling into a mindless pattern, but I do it because I'm really grateful for the sacrifice and generosity of these people.

When I write those notes, it does something for me; it reminds me of how blessed the Dream Center is to have such partners, and it makes me feel good to be able to thank them for their generosity.

> When you treat someone with respect and appreciation, you get the best they have to give.

And I know from my own experience that when you treat people with respect and appreciation, you get the best they have to give. People work better when they feel valued and loved.

GRATITUDE AT A GAS STATION

The Bible says we're to spread joy and gladness wherever we go, so I do my best to light up the room when I have the chance.

Some years ago when I was still pastoring in Davenport, I had a particular gas station that I always used. Every time I entered the convenience mart at the station, I was upbeat and affirming to the people working there. One day when I was at that station, I walked in to prepay for the gas and spent some time talking to the guy behind the counter. I didn't notice there was another person in the store looking for some items. It turned out he was a man from our church.

After I returned outside to pump my gas, the guy from our church went to pay for his items. The clerk, who was not a Christian and didn't know our church member, said, "You know, every time that guy comes in here, he just lights up this place. We feel so good afterward."

When our church member passed along that story, it really touched me, causing me to challenge myself to try to have that same uplifting effect every day on someone I encounter. I began to think of all the people I come across who would appreciate a kind and uplifting word for what they do: the girl making my drink at the coffee shop, the guy checking my luggage at airport security, the waitress at the restaurant. How often do they receive a sincere word of gratitude from those they serve?

The more I do this with people, the more I recognize that it doesn't take some well-rehearsed, clever dialogue to bring a smile to their faces. Eye contact and a simple "Hi. How are you doing today?" may be all it takes. It almost becomes a game: what can I do or say to make these people happier and lift their spirits?

One of my friends told me about something he consciously does every week. He lives a few thousand miles away from his parents, and they neither visit nor call him because they do not want to intrude on his life. So he takes a half hour each week to call or e-mail them, and he always spends a minute or two in those communications recalling some significant event from his life that they were responsible for and thanks them for loving and raising him.

He found out from one of his siblings—who, by the way, does not practice that kind of gratitude—how much it means to his parents. My friend admitted that he almost feels guilty that it means so much to them because it is so easy for him to express his genuine appreciation to them. But that's how simple and yet meaningful it can be to invest your half hours in spreading gratitude.

DON'T FORGET TO THANK GOD TOO!

On my way home from our church every day—not just Sundays, but every day—I spend my drive time reflecting on what happened that day and thank God for all the insights and influence that occurred.

On my way home after every sermon, I ponder what our church needs now—it's a kind of "preventive maintenance preaching" approach. I try to anticipate where we are headed and what that means for us both as a body of believers and for the individuals involved. I make a mental note of anything that needs to be corrected, any bad trends that are evident, or something we're neglecting. And I thank God for those revelations and opportunities.

If I am on the road, guest preaching at another church, I return to my hotel afterward and spend a half hour praising God for His involvement, for using me in that process, and for lessons He taught me from the experience.

The thirty minutes we invest in acknowledging God's presence and engagement in our lives and activities are a crucial factor in creating a permanent bond with Him. And I'm quite sure He prefers that kind of interaction over being treated like an eternal ATM machine. Don't you think He will be more responsive to our request if we have an ongoing relationship with Him, built on humility and gratitude, than if we simply implore Him to act on the spot?

And, by the way, if you feel you have nothing to be grateful for, check your pulse! If you find one, take a half hour to thank the Creator who gave you and sustains your life. That show of appreciation will undoubtedly reap positive dividends for you.

13

SLOW DOWN

Half-Hour Power Principle:
Step off your treadmill to get perspective.

Sometimes it's good to stop running and be quiet. I know that sounds countercultural.

These days we have become accustomed to keeping ourselves busy. Things like television programs, video games, the Internet, movies—it's all fun, but it comes at a price. What all that entertainment and activity does is anesthetize us to our world. If we keep ourselves busy enough, no matter how we do it, then we don't have to confront reality. We won't have to deal with the truth. We can take comfort in busyness and entertainment rather than deal with the tough situations of life.

It seems that half the nation's economy is tied to creating more noise and distractions, as if we believe that part of our daily responsibility is to add to the cacophony. We feel as if we are missing out on something if we aren't immersed in a blaze of sights and sounds. Tranquility is rarely our first option.

When we get in busy mode, we don't allow for the half hour we need to debrief ourselves to make sense of all the turbulence and challenges in our lives. For a lot of folks, the only time it's quiet and still is when they're trying to sleep. Maybe our unwillingness to include times of stillness, reflection, and self-debriefing is why millions of Americans have so much trouble getting a good night of sleep.

> We need to debrief ourselves to
> make sense of all the turbulence
> and challenges in our lives.

This may be a counterintuitive idea to embrace, but by slowing down to reflect, you may accomplish more than if you were to continue your normal course of relentless activity. You don't have to become a monk living in seclusion to experience life-changing times of quiet with God. If you are ready to listen—even for thirty minutes—He can connect with you regardless of the environment. He just wants you to take the initiative.

One of the most attractive qualities of Jesus was His ability to stay calm and unruffled in the midst of angst and chaos. Stillness and quiet are good conditions to experience and valuable qualities to cultivate.

It gets pretty easy in our marketing-driven, consumption-crazed culture to lose sight of what really matters and how blessed we are. One of the benefits of being still before God is the opportunity to reflect on how fortunate we are today—and to know what we are called to do and to be every day.

As novel as this may seem, incorporating silence, stillness, and meditation into our daily experience is not a new concept. Jesus modeled it for His followers two thousand years ago. Benedictine monks have been living in silence and stillness since the sixth century. They practice these disciplines because they believe that unnecessary noise and activity disrupt our ability to hear from God, to concentrate on Him, and often lead us to pursue our own desires rather than God's will.

Your life is probably pretty active. Experiencing intentional periods of quietness may be atypical for you—in fact, maybe you cannot even remember the last time you set aside a portion of your day to sit still and enjoy a time of rest and the intended absence of noise. But it is possible—and helpful—to designate a half hour of your time for such tranquility. You'll find that it is more productive than you expect.

God has great works in store for you if you will humble yourself before Him, prove yourself to be worthy in the small assignments, and commit yourself to pursuing His greatest dream for your life.

A Half-Hour Vision

A wonderful example of the benefits of becoming still is found in the life of Sharon Henning, who was a volunteer at our church before joining the staff. I had asked Sharon to take responsibility for our ministry to seniors, especially those with physical limitations. She was less than excited about the opportunity. Here's how she remembers our exchange and what eventually happened.

> I had not spent time on the prayer mountain before this, but Pastor Barnett had recently asked me to lead the bus ministry for the seniors in the congregation and community. I told him, "You've got to be kidding me. I don't know how to do any of that. I've never done anything remotely like that—ever. I love older people, but I'm not the right person for that job. I'm sorry, but there's no way."
>
> And he never stopped smiling; he just patted me on the shoulder and said, "You can do it. I know you can. You have it in you."
>
> So I decided to go up on the mountain and pray about this. I only had a half hour before I had to be at work. When I got to the top of the mountain, I was yelling at God and asking Him how in the world He thought I was going to do that ministry. I was pretty worked up about the whole thing.
>
> Sure enough, there I was, on the top of this mountain, and believe it or not, I couldn't see the city. As far as I could see, God gave me a vision. I saw elderly people in wheelchairs, as far as I could see.

The Lord spoke to me and said, *"I have called you to minister to them, so they will see Me and know Me. It won't be easy, but I'll be with you."*

[After such an experience] what can you say but yes?

That encounter took place almost two decades ago. Sharon is still with our church, and God has used her to build a world-class ministry to seniors. Today Sharon oversees ten wheelchair buses that we completely fill every weekend, special needs Sunday school classes, the training of dozens of volunteers to minister in fifty care centers around the city, a medical equipment lending closet for the community, a summer camp for those with special needs, a wealth of senior Bible studies, forums for seniors, and an annual Christmas pageant that the church performs with one night reserved for seniors. It's likely that those things would not exist today if Sharon had not been willing to be still long enough to let God reveal His vision for her life in such a dramatic fashion.

It only took a half hour. God can do miraculous things during such a fraction of time.

When was the last time you spent a half hour still and quiet in God's presence? What's stopping you from doing so today?

14

WHEN GOD CALLS... ANSWER "YES"

Half-Hour Power Principle:
Obeying God leads to satisfaction.

There really is no future in trying to talk God out of something! When He asks, rather than prolonging things, just obey and say yes.

After many failures in this area, I'm getting better at shortening the time and energy expanded between answering God with "What did you say?" or "You can't be serious?" to "Okay, let's do it."

> There really is no future in trying
> to talk God out of something!

One example of a slow start on my part—but eventually a good outcome—relates to the televangelist Jim Bakker. The financial abuses and subsequent collapse of Jim's ministry in the late 1980s resulted in a prison term for Jim. It was an ugly period for the church at large and a devastating episode in the lives of many people who lost money or faith as a result of the things that happened in regard to the PTL ministry.

During the time of Jim's imprisonment, I was reading my morning devotions when I encountered the passage that says, "For I was hungry, and you fed me. I was thirsty, and you gave me a drink. I was a stranger, and you invited me into your home. I was naked, and you gave me clothing. I was sick, and you cared for me. I was in prison, and you visited me."[13] As I was reading that portion, I was feeling pretty good about myself. I figured that through our work at the Dream Center I was feeding people, giving them drink, and providing housing. But in my spirit I felt uncomfortable about the phrase describing those in prison. Thinking about the terrific prison ministry we have at our church did not satisfy my inner discomfort. Then I felt that the Lord was telling me, *"I want you to go visit Jim Bakker."*

Immediately I began to compile a long list of reasons why that request made no sense whatsoever. I began the inner battle that sometimes occupies our minds when we feel a need to resist the call of God. *Man, that's all the way up there in Minnesota. It's cold up there. I don't really know Jim that well. Things are so busy right now at our church in Phoenix, and we're just getting the church and Dream Center in Los Angeles off the ground. It'd cost a bunch of money to fly up there and back, and nobody's going to reimburse me for that personal expense. Spending time with Jim in prison would be really uncomfortable. And if the media finds out that I was there to see him, it might not be good for my reputation.*

Right then the Lord spoke to me. I had an unmistakable impression from God: *"Well, your reputation isn't so hot anyway. Go see Jim Bakker."*

Okay. Yes Sir!

So after my half hour of dithering, I made the arrangements and flew to Minnesota to see Jim. When I walked in to the visitor's area where he was waiting for me, Jim ran to me and threw his arms around me. He was weeping, and he hung on to me for a bit before he said, "You know, nobody comes to visit me. Billy Graham has been here and now you."

Jim is an emotional guy, and I know the fact that he had been shunned by everyone hurt him deeply; that simple hug meant the world to him. I spent the next half hour talking and praying with Jim, and that began a long-term relationship that included our opportunity to minister to his estranged son and to later help Jim return to productive ministry.

It was cold in Minnesota, but I didn't notice because of that warm spot in my heart from blessing a brother in Christ...and saying "yes" to God (after a short delay) when He called!

"Do It!"

Do you become uncomfortable when you see a person standing by an intersection with a sign asking for money? The question that often goes through my mind is, *How do I know if this person has a legitimate need?* We've all read stories about full-time panhandlers who make a nice income from handouts.

Sorry to disappoint you, but I don't have an easy answer for this one. I may be a lifelong pastor who has given thousands of sermons, but the best advice I can give for such situations is "trust what the Holy Spirit whispers in your heart."

I remember one early morning I was sitting in front of a convenience store, deeply enjoying the "spiritual experience" of reading my morning newspaper and sipping coffee. A car pulled in next to me, and the driver beeped his horn. I was startled and a little annoyed. The reason I was having my coffee in the car was so I could have a little uninterrupted time with God! The guy motioned for me to roll down my window, and then he said, "Hey, I don't want to bother you, but could I borrow twenty dollars? I need to replace my tire, and I'm short twenty bucks. I'll pay you back this week." He motioned to a rear tire that did look low on air.

Talk about getting put on the spot! This was more in your face than somebody holding a sign by the road. The man did look a little ragged and stressed—but not that bad. And he was driving a car...

I struggled in my mind as we often do, wondering how I should respond. This was shaping up as one of the best scams I'd heard yet! Nevertheless, I sensed the internal whisper: *"Do it!"*

So as I reached for my wallet, I told the man that I was a pastor and asked that he come to our church the next Sunday—that would be enough repayment for me. "Just come up to me after the service and say hello. That's all you have to do," I said.

The man took the money and promised, "I'll be there—I promise!"

I looked for him that Sunday, but he didn't show up. And I looked for several Sundays with no success. So I forgot about it.

Then, a year later, a man met me at the altar. "Do you recognize me?" he asked.

"You do look familiar, but…"

"I'm the guy you gave the twenty dollars to a year ago for a tire. Well, today I came to your church, and just now I prayed and accepted Jesus. So the debt is paid, right?"

I gave him a hug and said, "Brother, that's not all that's paid. The debt for your sins was paid on Calvary, and that's the most important debt of all."

(But come to think of it, I'm not sure if he ever actually bought a tire—*just kidding!*)

My conclusion is that even if you're not totally sure what God is whispering, it's better to err toward generosity. We certainly have a God who is a tremendous giver and blesses us when we come with our hand outstretched.

We are the children of a heavenly Father who loves us so much! His plans for us always are for our good. That's why getting on board as quickly as possible when He asks us to do something is such a smart—make that *wise*—response. It's not always easy, but we need to…just do it!

Part 5

The Power of a Half Hour to

ADVANCE YOUR DREAMS

15

FOLLOW YOUR PASSION

Half-Hour Power Principle:
Your dreams are God's dreams for you.

Throughout my life I have seen many half hours used to foster someone's passion and dreams. Sometimes it involved taking risks; other times it involved simply a commitment to action. The results were usually humbling.

When the church in Los Angeles that my son Matthew and I were copastoring started to grow rapidly, we began searching for a nearby property that would allow expansion of the ministry. As the church grew, the congregation started buying all the houses on the neighboring blocks and managing its ministry from there. One day Matthew became aware of a huge, abandoned hospital campus that was for sale near the church, so he took me there to meet with the Catholic sisters who were in charge of selling the campus for the diocese that owned the property. They already had an excellent offer for the hospital from one of the big movie studios, but they really liked the fact that we were a ministry, so they wanted to give us a chance to place an offer.

Initially, the list price was $16 million. There was no way we could do that; we didn't have any money—only a vision of what God could do if we had a bigger facility. But pride reared its ugly head, and in front of Matthew I didn't want to look like I lacked faith. So I told myself that we would just examine the property, make a ridiculously low offer, and be done with it.

We walked through the fifteen-floor hospital building and the adjacent buildings. When we were done, the real estate broker asked, "What do you think?"

I smiled and said, "It's really wonderful."

She pressed on, "Do you want to buy it?"

I admitted, "Well, yes, we'd love to, but we can't afford it."

She paused and then said, "Make me an offer."

This was the moment I had anticipated, when I'd propose an absurdly low figure, and everyone would leave. "I'll give you $3.9 million for it," I said.

That did not generate the reaction I'd expected. There was no look of astonishment, no gasp of embarrassment, no laugh at the silliness of my offer. The broker just paused again, then said, "I'll take it."

We didn't have that kind of money. Matthew's church was filled with drug addicts, alcoholics, homeless people, and hookers—it was not a big tithing crowd. Getting a property worth more than $25 million for just under $4 million was the steal of the century—unless you only have a couple hundred thousand saved up.

But over the next few months we managed to pull together a half million dollars, which was enough to close the deal. But then we had to come up with the remaining $3.4 million in the next eighteen months. We had no idea how that would happen.

During the next sixteen months we were able to squirrel away $1.4 million, which we thought was remarkable but was still $2 million short. The contract stated that if we did not pay them in full on the final date, the entire property would revert to them, and our previous payment of $1.9 million would not be refunded.

Meanwhile, back at my church in Phoenix, almost everyone was supportive of my efforts to help Matthew and his congregation move into the new campus—with one notable exception: an influential man who was a friend of mine. He said he loved me so much that he couldn't let me invest myself in that new campus—that the burden of raising the money and renovating the abandoned buildings would be too much for me. His concern for me was moving, but, of course, I had to move forward with this incredible opportunity.

My God-given passion to help others was fully activated, but we needed a miracle. And God loves to fulfill the dreams in us He birthed.

One day this same man came to see me and said he wanted to go with me to LA to see the Dream Center. I had been avoiding him because I didn't want the conflict, and I was even less excited about taking a road trip with this guy and having to listen to his negative comments about the new campus. But he was a good man, a friend who really cared about me, so we made the journey out West.

> God loves to fulfill the
> dreams in us He birthed.

I took him on a half-hour tour of the campus and explained what we envisioned for the ministry. Tears welled up in his eyes—and he was not a crying kind of guy. Afterward I took him back to his hotel. That evening I was scheduled to pick him up again and accompany him to the evening service. He called ahead of time and requested that I come early so we could grab a bowl of soup together before the service. So we got some soup, and before he started eating he began to weep.

"I've never seen anything like this in my life," he sobbed. "And I know you must be up against the wall financially for this property." He quietly wrote a check for a million dollars. That was the first million-dollar check I ever received. Then he said, "I just called my son. He wants to meet with you next week."

Sure enough, the following week I flew back to LA to meet his son and give the thirty-minute tour. And his son gave me another check for a million dollars. Neither of them had any idea that we were right up against our deadline and had been short…$2 million.

Apparently, I give a killer thirty-minute tour!

Seriously, God overcame the impossible through those two men—and blessed us with a campus that has enabled us to pursue our passion for helping the people our society has discarded.

Our God is amazing. Spend thirty minutes with Him on a regular basis exploring how He wants to encourage your passions to do great things with Him!

16

PREPARE FOR SUCCESS

Half-Hour Power Principle:
Preparation includes ample perspiration.

Whenever you see someone doing a complicated task with grace and ease, you can be sure without a doubt that the person has spent countless hours in preparation. Getting prepared is not the glamorous part, no matter what the task may be. But there will be no glamour realized unless you do sufficient preparation.

Champions prepare themselves for victory. Experts invest in preparation. Figuring out what it takes to come out on top and then putting in the sweat and toil to get there is what distinguishes winners from losers in life.

> Getting prepared is not the glamorous
> part, no matter what the task may be.

How many times have you read about garage bands that toiled for ten or fifteen years in grungy clubs before they released a hit song that launched them to "overnight success"? It's a more common occurrence than you might imagine. In our instant-gratification society we downplay all the hard work it takes to reach goals, but that does not change the need for a commitment to readiness.

How many people have you met who think they have a book inside of their head—a story that they should write because it would be a bestseller? One well-known author speaking at a recent writers' conference estimated that about one out of every five people he meets at book signings tells him that they have a great book inside that is waiting to get out and wow the world. The author went on to say they may be right—but we won't know until those people do the hard work of preparing to write their potential bestseller. He argued that what makes or breaks a book is what is done to pave the way for its success, before the first word is written: the research, concept testing, outlining, and other elements of preparation that set apart the great writers from the wannabe writers.

I experienced that in getting ready to write this book. When the idea for the book became clear in my mind, I began asking friends for their reactions or suggestions. Ken Blanchard, the internationally revered management authority, who coauthored one of the best-selling books of all-time (*The One Minute Manager*) and has written more than sixty books, was one who reflected on this book with me. Ken responded favorably to the idea before adding his warning: "The problem is there are a lot of guys like you who get a great idea, but they never follow through. I'm in business because of guys who have a terrific book concept that could sell a million copies, but they never do it."

Those words were a wake-up call; Ken could have been talking about me! So I started setting aside thirty minutes a day to prepare for the writing of this book. Sometimes the half hour was while waiting for my flight at the airport. Other times it was a half hour while sitting in the waiting room at my doctor's office. This book is the result of many half hours of preparation involving periods of study, reflection, and note taking. All of that information was then organized and developed into the manuscript.

Even if this book never becomes a bestseller, I know I can be proud of it because it represents my best effort to communicate the importance of the theme—and that was made possible by practicing the thirty-minute concept in preparation for the writing phase.

Different Types of Preparation

There are three types of preparation that you need to do if you want to maximize your potential and ultimately achieve success. Earlier, we examined how you can use your half hours to be *spiritually* prepared to meet the challenges of each day and life. But you must also be prepared *mentally* and *physically* to produce your best work.

The idea behind preparing your mind and heart is to have a viable perspective on the task at hand. Sometimes that means getting your mind in tune with your motivation. For instance, before I enter a counseling session with an individual or couple, I remind myself that I can either mindlessly piddle through the half hour or I can enter the room intent on helping change a life. Mindless piddling simply requires me to show up; the second approach demands that I think through my role, the conversational boundaries, the strategic goals and assignments, and so forth. Which kind of counselor would you want?

Your preparation can have a lasting effect on people. When my boys were little, we played a lot of basketball together. We'd make up shooting games to see who would win. Basketball players get famous for making dramatic shots, but the statistics show that players actually miss a majority of their shots.

One day, after one of my sons threw up a potential game-winning shot and missed, I got the rebound and then called a timeout to explain something important: "Boys, what matters most in life is not whether you miss a shot. You're going to miss a lot of shots in life; we all do. What matters most is what you do after you miss a shot. The greatest basketball players are the rebounders—the ones who give their team another opportunity to score! You may have a great team, but if you don't have a Bill Russell, Wilt Chamberlain, or Charles Barkley to snag the rebound that gives you another chance to shoot and win, you won't get far."

I wanted my sons to capture the mental image of the preparation and practice it takes to get to the place where a winning shot is possible. Their perspective needed to be refocused.

There are, of course, many different ways of sharpening your perspective and getting ready to accomplish your goals. I am often impressed by the lengths that athletes go to in preparing their minds and hearts for competition.

Muhammad Ali was famous for his prefight psych-up ritual. After he was dressed and taped, his trainers would offer a few parting words of encouragement and then leave him alone to meditate until it was time to enter the ring. When he emerged, he was like a caged animal, ready to rumble. He sneered and made faces of disgust at his opponent. He would yell insults and taunts at his rival with phrases such as, "I am the greatest," "You're a chump," "I'm gonna whup your [butt]," "Nobody can beat me," and "I'm going to float like a butterfly and sting like a bee." He was psyching himself up and psyching out his opponent.

We all have different tasks to perform in order to fulfill our unique calling from God. Thankfully, mine has nothing to do with punching people in the face! (I have to admit, though, I always laughed when I heard Ali's nonchalant description of his job: "It's just a job," he pointed out. "Grass grows, birds fly, waves pound sand, I beat people up.")[14]

But the process is the same, regardless of the job.

During the week leading up to any given Sunday morning, I have times when I begin to prepare mentally for the chance to share some truth from God's Word with my audience. I pray for guidance, strength, confidence, and wisdom.

A GREAT INVESTMENT

If something is meaningful to you, don't you want to do whatever you can to maximize your potential performance? If so, then prepare to make the most of the moment. Whether that means spending a half hour becoming better informed, refining your skills, building valuable relationships, inviting God to be part of your efforts, or thanking Him for how He has enabled you, getting psyched up for the challenge, enlisting other people to be in your corner, or studying some best practices to draw from, the fact is that you can improve your chances of success by preparing your mind and heart. If this becomes a habit in your life, you will discover that life becomes more enjoyable, more productive, and more meaningful.

It only takes a few half hours devoted to preparation.

17

MAKE A CAREER "WORK"

Half-Hour Power Principle:
Boost productivity with thirty-minute meetings.

All of us face problems each day. The solutions are sometimes obvious, but then there are the stumpers that throw us for a loop. One of the life lessons I've gleaned is that I won't always have the solution to the problems I face, but someone I know has the answer I'm looking for.

One of the most consistent sources of treasure in our organization is the half-hour lunches our staff has together. I intentionally promote them spending those half hours with each other, not because I want them to become cliquish, but because they cross-pollinate when they're together. That insight has been driven home by personal experience. I cannot begin to count the number of times I head to lunch with one of them and lay out a challenge I'm wrestling with, only to find that they help me develop the solution I've been seeking.

You don't have to hire a high-priced consultant to study your challenges and issue a report; some good, old-fashioned conversation with friends and colleagues can put you back on a productive track within thirty minutes.

When I'm stymied, the members of the church team at Phoenix First Assembly are my ideal lunch mates because they know my context and can be trusted to keep the matter confidential. You have people like that in your life who can help boost your creative problem-solving capacity, thanks to a half hour spent together at lunch.

> You have people like that in your
> life who can help boost your
> creative problem-solving capacity.

It doesn't have to be accomplished over food, though. When you face a bump in the road, sometimes it just takes a short conversation with someone of like heart to come up with a solution.

THIRTY-MINUTE MEETINGS

A friend of mine was a lay leader at a Presbyterian church. He was a successful and very busy businessman, so it was always difficult for him to carve time out of his schedule for the monthly church meetings, but he dutifully did so. However, when he was invited to join the elder board, he told the committee that he would do so under one condition: that at the two-hour mark, he would walk out of each meeting. When asked why, he told them that if they couldn't make their decisions in two hours, they probably had not sufficiently prepared and were just wasting time doing what should have been done prior to the meeting. Thinking that he was joking, the committee assured him such a strange idea was fine.

At the two-hour mark of his first meeting, realizing that the group was nowhere close to completing the night's agenda, my friend gathered up his papers and quietly left the meeting. As he got up to walk out, the arguing around the table stopped and eleven pairs of eyes silently watched him depart. Each of the next three months, the same thing happened. Finally, during the meeting in his fifth month on the board, it appeared that the agenda would be completed after close to two hours, so my friend stayed a few extra minutes until the end. The meetings every month thereafter were finished within two hours.

The entire process of how those meetings were run and prepared for had changed because of his insistence on the leaders' adequate preparation and discussion management to ensure the efficient use of everyone's time.

I guess we've just taken his approach further, limiting our staff meetings to a half hour. There are times when we have to meet longer, of course, but those are the exceptions, not the norm. Half-hour meetings can produce enormous dividends if you are dedicated to respecting people's time and intelligence.

Many of our leaders have adopted the habit of running half-hour meetings. One of our pastors, J. J. Hayes, recently described her process of pulling together all her workers for thirty minutes each Sunday morning and briefing everyone on the plan of action for the week. All of the staff members get to add their two cents to the discussion, but they know they have to be prepared and succinct. That short meeting is an efficient way of enabling everyone to prepare for his or her responsibilities and to support everyone else's efforts that week.

J. J. came to us from the corporate world and had never run meetings that way before. Now she laughs about it:

> It's funny because it's a very "old school" way to run a meeting.
> There's nothing fancy about what we do or how we do it. But that
> half hour has brought our team so much closer together. Most of
> them already know what's coming up because they get other com-
> munications from us preceding the meeting, and I try to meet with
> each of them regularly for coffee or something small that takes a half
> hour, to stay in touch. But they enjoy the weekly meeting for the
> fellowship and that half hour of looking into each other's eyes, and
> the half hour of attention they get that makes them feel like they're
> in the know. They are better at their jobs because they know what to
> expect and how to prepare. It's kind of fun.

My longtime assistant, Lynn Lane, oversees our annual event for pastors, now known as the Dream Conference (it used to be called the Pastor's School).

It probably would be considered normal to have a series of long meetings prior to an event that draws thousands of pastors from around the nation, but Lynn uses a few half-hour meetings in which she gets down to business and refuses to waste people's time. She sees those times as mentoring opportunities, preparing people to improve what they do for the conference from year to year.

"During those thirty minutes, I try to build up people, mentor them, encourage them, maybe teach them something simple but useful, remind them of their purpose," Lynn explained. "I always exhort them to be positive, to smile, to spend time with God, and to keep records of how everything went so they can improve next year. I am setting them up for success. It's thirty minutes of valuable mentoring."

Aaron Dunn is the pastor in charge of our outreach and church life activities. He has about fourteen leaders who report to him in that capacity. There is probably nobody on our team who is more committed to the half-hour concept than Aaron. He talks freely about how the concept has worked for him, both before he started serving at Phoenix First Assembly as well as in his ministry with us.

> Before coming to Phoenix First, I worked in the phone industry
> managing people. I was a trainer, coaching people in Best Buy and
> other retail box stores to sell products. I used the half-hour process
> there. I got in the habit of having a weekly half-hour meeting with
> my supervisor, then I would go into a store and meet for a half hour
> with the store manager, another half hour with the sales manager, and
> then a half hour with his group of employees. Everything was done on
> that half-hour scale: five minutes to prepare, twenty minutes to meet,
> and then five minutes to debrief myself and write notes for future
> reference. For me to bring that approach into the culture here at the
> church was real easy to do because I had been conditioned to it before
> I started here.
>
> I stepped into this role and currently have fourteen different

directors that report to me, all related to the outreach ministries and church life ministries here. My first thought upon arriving was, *Man, this is a huge undertaking. How should I attack this?* Then I started to solve the problem by asking myself, *How do you eat an elephant? One bite at a time.* So from the very beginning, I instituted half-hour meetings with all my directors. Every Monday is filled with half-hour meetings. I live and die by those half-hour meetings, the one-on-one exchanges with each director. A half hour gives me just enough time. With fourteen direct reports I have a lot to do, so I can't give each of them more than a half hour to get the week going.

For me, a half hour is the right amount of time to get the information I need to do my job and to empower them and to help them as leaders. Those half hours are tightly structured, in three ten-minute blocks. We start with ten minutes concerning their list of priorities and activities, including family and personal matters. That first ten minutes is for them. The next ten minutes is for me to cover some things I've prepared for them, either on a professional or personal level. It's my chance to get some answers about the direction and strategy of their ministry and projects. The final ten minutes is for ministry development and career development, where we focus on growth and opportunities.

If I miss one of our meetings, I really feel like I'm out of the loop and I'm not empowering them. We have 275 different ministries here; you could easily feel like you were out of the loop, out of the spotlight, or that you had no opportunity for input. But their half hour with me allows me to represent them in the executive meetings or my half-hour weekly meetings with Pastor Luke [Barnett]. They feel like they have a voice because in our half hour together, I get information from them, and then I become their voice. I'm a better advocate for the people that I'm leading. It's vital to me, to them, and to the overall success of the church's ministry.

The Worry Box

Every day I seem to encounter at least one problem that I cannot solve. I know that's common. But what I see many people do is fritter away the rest of their day grappling with that problem. Nothing else gets done.

Here's my way of handling those tough problems: I put them in my "worry box." I've got too much to accomplish in any given day to be shut down by a single problem, so I take a piece of paper, write out the problem, and put it in a special tray on my desk that is reserved for such matters, a tray that we literally call the Worry Box. My commitment is that at 4:30 p.m., toward the end of the workday, I return to my office, read through those pages that describe the vexing obstacles, and work on them for thirty minutes—after having spent a productive day solving all the other problems that leaders have to address.

Some might think all I'm doing is procrastinating. Not at all! What I have found is that by later in the afternoon, most of those problems have already taken care of themselves or been solved. Many of them, it turns out, were not worth worrying about. The ones that remain can then get my undivided attention until conclusions are reached.

You've probably had situations in the past where you took a few minutes and figured out how to resolve some difficult situation. Imagine if you were more intentional about your challenges each day, setting aside a half hour at a certain time of day to address those matters. If your experience parallels mine, you'll discover that the power of a half hour set aside for such problem solving frees you up to accomplish more during the rest of the day.

18

ACTIVATE
YOUR CREATIVITY

Half-Hour Power Principle:
Be creative...like your heavenly Dad.

Have you produced something artistic or purely creative? It's not only hard work, but it is difficult to sustain that creative edge. However, with some focused attention, amazing creativity can be birthed or even executed in a half hour.

A man I know began one of the largest and most influential charitable organizations in the country. He became a popular radio personality and then branched into writing books to spread his message further. Over the last thirty years, his books have sold more than twenty million copies in this country and millions more overseas. He has won just about every publishing award available in Christian circles for his insightful and practical books.

I was surprised to learn that he writes his books at a very deliberate pace: one page every day. He gets up early in the morning, when his mind is fresh and his energy level is high, and after his devotional time he labors over a single page of content—about a half hour or so each morning. After eight or nine months of that process, he has a complete manuscript, which he then edits before submitting to his publisher.

My son Matthew has a similar approach to his writing. Besides leading the Dream Center and church in Los Angeles, Matthew regularly writes blog entries that focus on a slice of his life to encourage or challenge people through his experiences. He devotes a half hour to those simple and practical lessons that have helped thousands of people.

EXPRESS YOURSELF FOR HIS GLORY

When you have something to express to God, use some creative gift He has given you, whether it is the ability to paint or write or sing or draw—just do it! If you put thirty minutes into conveying that idea to God, you have done something special. And you never know when the Lord might choose to use that gift in a way you never expected.

During a portion of our church services, we sometimes have people express their worship by using their talent for painting. Some of these are professional artists, while others would be considered hobbyists, but all of them use their art as a way of communicating deeply felt emotions. They have easels, canvases, brushes and palettes of paints, and a half hour to create their masterpieces as gifts to God. For many artistic individuals, it presents a chance to empty themselves of their deepest but otherwise inexpressible feelings to their heavenly Father. It is their best means of communicating their most profound emotions, insights, yearnings, and gratitude to God.

> When you have something to express to God,
> use some creative gift He has given you.

One of my friends is Darlene Zschech, the gifted worship leader from Hillsong ministry in Australia. Hillsong was preparing to cut a new album of worship songs when they were informed at the last minute that the fellow who was going to be the musical director for the project had canceled. He was the guy who had all the songs written, chosen, and arranged, so this was a big blow to senior pastor Brian Houston and his team. Brian was quite discouraged for a while until someone told him that Darlene had written a song. Now that was not anything to get excited about at the time—since she was working as a church secretary.

With few other options, the team asked Darlene about her song. "Well, I don't know if it's any good or not," she told them. They asked her to sing it so they could decide if it was good enough to consider. So she started singing the song she had written, "Shout to the Lord." The rest, as they say, is history. It is one of the most widely sung worship songs in the world, earning Darlene global recognition and a Dove nomination for Songwriter of the Year. It has been on the Billboard Top 100 songs and was sung by the contestants on *American Idol* (twice). It was not a moment she expected, but when the time arrived, Darlene was ready to use her gift to glorify God.

19

SUSTAIN HOPE

Half-Hour Power Principle:
Hope results from God's grace and your effort.

We all need to have a strong sense of hope in our lives. Without it, even our dreams will wither.

So how do we keep our hearts brimming with hope?

On my journey with God, I've discovered several strategies for energizing hope. First, reading His Word every day instructs, reinforces, and encourages me. In a half hour I can read several psalms, which demonstrate the power of God to overcome the world, or passages from any of the other Bible books God has preserved for us.

Second, when I take a half hour to ponder my salvation—the freedom purchased for me at the cost of Jesus's life and the eternal opportunities promised to me—the immediate attitudes that emerge are hope, joy, gratitude, and peacefulness. I never want to take for granted the incredible sacrifice that He made for me, or lose sight of the fact that God tells us that His plan for us provides a future and hope.[15]

Third, when I spend my time praying that the Holy Spirit will have complete control of my life, hope abounds within me. God honors that prayer, and the burdens of the day are no longer mine; there is hope in the release of control to the omnipotent One. And that, of course, enables me to recognize the opportunities and the impact that He provides, as I described earlier. When you consider that provision, hope swells within your heart.

Hope is one of the greatest gifts that God gives us. But sometimes you have to work at getting it into your head and heart. Circumstances sometimes overwhelm us, and as a result we lose sight of the big picture of life. Learning how to restore hope in our hearts is an invaluable skill.

> Hope is one of the greatest
> gifts that God gives us.

I don't struggle with a sense of hopelessness very often; working on having an attitude of hope and joy seems to block out the blues. But every once in a while I succumb—but not for long, because I have a few tried and trusted ways of defeating feelings of despair. You can too, if you invest a half hour of time into recalibrating your attitude.

ACCEPT ENCOURAGEMENT FROM OTHERS

Sometimes it's easier to give than to receive. That can be true of affirmation too.

Not long after I first arrived in Phoenix and had started the church, we had a janitor who was a legend. Even though we were a downtown church, he kept the buildings immaculate. When I announced we were going to run buses and pick up poor and disadvantaged kids from around town, everybody just held their breath, wondering how the janitor was going to respond. Some people predicted a war between the two of us. I was just doing what I felt God wanted me to do.

At first there was no problem. The bus ministry continued to grow and one day, when we had reached four buses going into the community, the janitor came to see me. "Pastor," he said, "I know that maybe you're wondering how I feel about bringing in all these bused kids because everybody knows I've kept this place in good condition." His voice softened and tears filled his eyes as he continued. "Years ago when I was at the big Baptist church in Cincinnati, we had buses and brought in kids from all over the city. Since I moved out here, I have prayed for years that God would send somebody here that would run buses to reach the children." He went on to explain what it meant to him. Then I gave him my vision for what the bus ministry could do, and soon we both had tears in our eyes.

That man became a close friend of mine, and that little thirty-minute talk encouraged me to keep going forward for God. All he did was affirm my efforts to be obedient to God, regardless of the consequences. We saw that ministry expand to some forty buses bringing in kids every week. His supportive words were an important factor in the growth of that program.

Find Someone to Encourage

Whenever I'm faced with a personal hope deficit, I force my attention onto something that makes my spirit soar. For instance, I support several kids in Christian school. When I get discouraged, I drive by their school and say, "Just look at that play yard. I get to be a part of that." Thinking about how different the lives of those children are because I get the privilege of helping them gets me excited. What could be better than knowing you play some role in the betterment of another person's life? I imagine who those children will grow up to be, and I get filled with hope—for them, for the country, and for the kingdom of God.

> The best way to escape that pit of despair is to call up somebody and encourage that person.

Sometimes your health can get the best of you. A couple of years ago I needed a heart operation, because I had a valve that was leaking. That was very discouraging for me, because I work at staying healthy. Besides running long distances, I exercise regularly and I love playing basketball games with the young men in our church. (No, they don't let me win, and they don't give the old man a break—I wouldn't stand for it!) During my recovery from the heart surgery, I became depressed for one of the few times in my life. It was terrible. But I found out that the best way to escape that pit of despair was to call up somebody and encourage that person. Even though that's not the easiest thing to do—addressing other people's problems can be a bit sensitive or emotional—in the end it winds up boosting the spirits of both of us.

Sometimes I counsel with people and, after helping them work through a marriage issue or some emotional trauma, I finally get to leave the building at 11:00 p.m., and I think, *How great was that? While other people slept, I got to help somebody.* That's the best feeling in the world: knowing that I helped somebody. By helping others, I help myself and restore my sense of hope.

Part of my morning prayer regimen is to pray, "God, please help me to help somebody today. I don't want to waste Your time or the opportunities You have reserved for me. I'm going to try to make my life really count today. Please bless my efforts." At the end of each day, as part of my final prayer, I ask myself, *Now did I help anybody today?* If I didn't, I ask God to forgive me and to strengthen and prepare me to do better tomorrow.

Hope's Foundation

These days people talk a lot about living in the moment, not thinking about the future. I understand that, and there is biblical support for that mentality—to a point. The other side of that coin is that you can only maintain a mind-set of letting go of fears and anxieties if you have an attitude permeated with hope. But hope for its own sake is ignorant; that hope must be based on something—or Someone. That Someone is the God of creation.

One of the most powerful scripture passages to retain is Romans 5:3–5. Those verses spell it out succinctly for us:

> We can rejoice, too, when we run into problems and trials, for we
> know that they help us develop endurance. And endurance devel-
> ops strength of character, and character strengthens our confident
> hope of salvation. And this hope will not lead to disappointment.
> For we know how dearly God loves us, because he has given us the
> Holy Spirit to fill our hearts with his love. (NLT)

You need hope when life gets rough, but what is that hope based on? If you tie your hope to the power and love of God, then you can endure the difficulties of life, become a person of character who recognizes your own insufficiency without Christ, and have an unshakable hope because Jesus is at the center of your existence. Powered by God's Spirit, you can handle anything, from victory to adversity. Hope in Christ and in God's Word provides the perspective that empowers you to overcome every obstacle in life.

The Bible also informs us that such hope produces other attributes within us: courage, joy, confidence, and comfort.[16] Armed with those cornerstones, your life will never be the same and you need fear nothing.

Part 6

The Power of a Half Hour to
IMPROVE YOUR
RELATIONSHIPS

BLESS OTHERS

Half-Hour Power Principle:
You exist for other people.

I think Jesus wants us to build people up. When the religious leaders asked Him what the most important commandment was, He informed them that it was to fully love God and people. If you study His life, you discover that Jesus's form of love was not an empty verbal expression or a flimsy emotion. Jesus was a man of action, and when He described love, it was about taking action that made people's lives better.

There's no better feeling in the world than knowing that you did something that built up somebody else. Whether it's a word of affirmation, an act of kindness, a physical expression of love, a sacrificial gift given, or the commitment of your time to someone else's life, the value of that effort is immeasurable.

> There's no better feeling in the world
> than knowing that you did something
> that built up somebody else.

The beauty of building up people is that you can have a lifelong positive impact on somebody in just thirty minutes. I know because people have done it for me, and I've done it for them.

One time a high school boy came in for an appointment. I asked him why he wanted to visit, and he blushed and began to stammer. I could tell he had something important on his heart to say, but he couldn't get the words out. After a few painful minutes of trying to converse, the young man finally blurted out, "Pastor Tommy, I love you." Then he leaped to his feet and ran from my office.

I ran after him and asked, "Have you ever told someone you loved them before?"

"No sir," he said, and took off.

Man, did that make my day! I felt great, but I sensed that saying he loved me made the young man feel even greater.

One of the foundational perspectives of my life is that I love people. Yes, it is true that we are all sinners and our nature has been negatively tainted by the world, but I choose to believe in the potential of people to make good decisions and become better human beings. That attitude enables me to serve people in ways that some consider foolish, but it is the same belief that motivated Jesus to surrender everything for your sake—and mine.

Over the years I have had more than my fair share of experiences in which people have burned me. I've been lied to, stolen from, gossiped about, cheated, stabbed in the back—and I bet you have too. But I know that I make mistakes too, and I realize that those indefensible choices are part of being human. Sin, properly handled and wisely understood, does not diminish the potential that God has placed in each of us.

I've sometimes thought that if I had not been called into ministry as a pastor and preacher, I would have enjoyed the life of a politician. Granted, that's not something you hear very often these days, but political officials are called to be public servants who can make a big difference in the world. They have the ability to inspire people to live more meaningfully and productively and to facilitate conditions that enable us to be the best we can be. But even without being a government official, you and I have a responsibility to live as servants, constantly seeking the optimal means of blessing God and other people.

Fortunately, I've been able to devote my life to ministry. During that time I cannot count the number of half-hour meetings I've had with members of my church who asked if they could start a new ministry venture as part of our church. Honestly, not many of them had the qualifications to lead a ministry. Surprisingly few of them had the experience to suggest that they would be effective at mobilizing people around their vision. But I believe in people—perhaps because I look at myself and realize I'm not qualified to accomplish most of the things the Lord has allowed me to do, either!

Who are the people in your life that, if you gave them a focused half hour of your time, you could show your love by encouraging them to pursue their dreams?

If somebody approaches me and is passionate about a particular form of ministry, I almost never turn that person down. Our church is organized in a way that enables us to support people in their efforts. Some of them fail, and some of them make it—and it is amazing how often the people I thought would fall flat are the ones who emerge victorious, and the ones I was sure would succeed are the ones who miss the mark. I don't want to be the guy who prevents someone from doing what God called him or her to do. Just as God believed in me enough to save me and send me, so do I want to be supportive of everyone who desires to serve the Lord and His people.

THIRTY-MINUTE BLESSINGS

I think one of the most important life principles a person can learn is the fact that God blesses us so that we can bless others.[17] One of the surprises that comes from that lifestyle is the joy of knowing that you have made someone else's life better. It's hard to bless others when your attitude is wrong, but it's just as hard to have a bad attitude when you are busy blessing people.

That is one of the things I try to encourage my staff to do.

One of my long-time associates, Sharon Henning, talks about how my regular encouragement to take advantage of half hours has led her to plan her daily schedule with an eye toward identifying available half hours and making the most of that free time. Sometimes she'll head to the mountain to pray; other times she gets on the phone to assist individuals in need; on other occasions she heads over to the senior-care center to help the staff there. Once you get the mind-set that your time is a resource that can bless others, blessing others becomes a wonderful habit.

Sometimes blessing others has life-or-death implications. At the church in Los Angeles, a woman named Maria benefitted from the Dream Center's Adopt-a-Block program. Every Saturday our teams visit their designated neighborhood blocks, doing whatever needs to be done to lend a helping hand, to provide much-needed food and clothing, and most of all, to share the love of Jesus Christ. Sometimes they mow lawns, paint, or repair appliances. But building relationships and inviting the neighbors to church is Adopt-a-Block's first priority.

Maria was a very quiet person. Although the Dream Center team visited her every week, she rarely said much about herself. She was always polite, but it wasn't often that anyone saw her smile, and even then her eyes never seemed to lose their sadness. The team learned that she was a single mother from Central America, and it was evident that she and her two children lived in poverty.

After several months Maria finally found the courage to attend a church service, and on that first visit she went forward and received Jesus Christ as her Savior. Everyone who knew her was ecstatic.

From that time on, visits with her were warmer and less awkward, but still Maria never lost her shyness and reserve.

One Saturday when the team knocked at Maria's door, nobody answered. They persisted for several minutes, until finally a neighbor appeared. The woman walked over with an uncertain expression on her face. "Haven't you heard?" she asked. "Maria was killed yesterday."

"Killed? What do you mean?" The Adopt-a-Block team members looked at each other in horror.

The neighbor nodded mutely but seemed reluctant to tell them more. Just then another more talkative neighbor arrived and recounted the terrible story. Maria's boyfriend had become angry with her and had pushed her in front of a moving car. She died instantly.

Maria's mother came from New York to Los Angeles for the funeral, and the Dream Center provided the facilities, food, and volunteer help necessary to make the occasion as pleasant as possible. The distraught mother wept inconsolably during the service. Afterward she spoke to my son Matthew. "Maria didn't talk to you much—I know that because she didn't talk much to anybody," she said. "But she wrote me a letter about you. She said you were the only friends she had in Los Angeles. Every week she looked forward to you coming to her door. She always dreamed that she would find friends here, and because of you, she did. Thank you for being there for my daughter."

As tragic as Maria's death was, we all agreed that she had found an even better friendship than anyone at the Dream Center could possibly provide: she had found Jesus, and now she was with Him for all eternity.

Those thirty-minute weekly visits from friends who loved Maria made all the difference.

Love is limitless. You can never lose love by giving it away. I decided long ago to start giving love away all the time—I call this enlarging your circle of love so that nobody is on the outside. An amazing thing happened! My capacity to love grew. My experience of love grew. The feeling of love expanded inside of me. The more I loved others, the more I was able to love them, and as a side benefit, I received more love in return.

Love is like a superfood! Nothing fills people with energy and strength quite like it does.

Make sure you are giving more than your share away.

21

CONNECT WITH IMPACT

Half-Hour Power Principle:
Good friendships require time...over time.

There may not be a better application of the power of a half hour than in relationships.

Think about the people who are part of your inner circle. Chances are good that they did not become your close friends overnight. The depth of your relationships with them took time to build. You had to invest a lot of energy, ideas, commitment, face time—all sorts of resources go into building a genuine friendship.

Even with people who are good friends but not in your inner circle, investing regular segments of time in those relationships is critical. The more intentional you are about using your half hours wisely, the more likely you will be to develop a solid community of relationships founded on your willingness to devote time to those people.

> All sorts of resources go into
> building a genuine friendship.

One of the people I work most closely with is Gary Blair. He travels with me all over the world, helping me in myriad ways. Gary tells the story of a time before he came to the church to work with me. He had lost his job in Phoenix and was going through a difficult time. After numerous failed attempts at landing another job, he wound up accepting a position in the oil fields of Oklahoma. He and his wife, Suzi, knew nobody in that state, so it was a hard and lonely transition for them.

They rented an apartment that had a pool in the middle of the complex. While most of the other residents kept to themselves, one couple who lived in a unit on the other side of the complex met the Blairs at the pool and befriended them. The husband, Randy, tried repeatedly to establish some common ground with Gary so they could deepen their relationship, but Gary was oblivious, still mired in his own funk. Randy and his wife, Jeannie, had a young child that they'd bring to the pool frequently, and Suzi spent a lot of time with Jeannie and the baby.

Suzi desperately wanted a baby, but they had not been able to have one, and with their financial issues, now wasn't a good time to start a family. It was a period fraught with tensions for both of them.

Even though Gary did not make much of an effort to know Randy, he regularly observed his neighbor and was secretly envious of the peace and purpose that Randy seemed to have in his life. One especially memorable episode was when Randy took a bunch of groceries he'd bought, as well as some from his own pantry, to give to another family living in the apartment complex. Gary later found out that both the husband and wife in that couple had lost their jobs and were struggling to stay afloat. Such sacrificial compassion was a real dilemma for Gary; he was captivated by it, but at the same time he didn't know what to make of it.

Eventually Gary and Suzi returned to Phoenix, but all the pressures they lived with had jeopardized their relationship. They had a serious disagreement soon after their return. As a kind of peace offering, Gary voluntarily attended the church Suzi was attending, although he was not a Christian and had no interest in church. He visited a Sunday school class where he listened intently as a teacher gave a half-hour teaching on the responsibilities of a husband and father. Since

Gary had never before heard such information, it really shook him up—and compelled him to return week after week.

Eventually, touched by the things he was learning and the different life views and behavior of the people he met at the church, he accepted Christ as his Savior and experienced a remarkable transformation. He has been a consistent and significant blessing to me as well as to many others ever since.

What intrigues me about Gary's story is that it began with Randy consistently investing thirty minutes or less trying to befriend Gary. The seeds Randy planted in Gary's life took years to bear fruit, and Randy personally never saw that fruit. But I see it every day as I work with Gary and watch him help me and so many other people.

Randy, wherever you are, that was a bunch of half hours well spent. Thank you!

22

STRENGTHEN MARRIAGE

Half-Hour Power Principle:
Thirty-minute encounters benefit every marriage.

Marriage may be a sacred institution ordained by God, but He sure didn't make it easy. I have devoted countless half hours—in a wide variety of situations—to the health and well-being of our marriage.

Marriage is a challenge for anyone, but even small investments in communication and in conflict resolution can vastly improve the health of your covenant relationship.

Our marriage got off to a pretty rocky start. My wife comes from a background very different from mine. Marja was born in Helsinki, Finland. Her dad was killed in the Winter War (a conflict the Soviet Union initiated against Finland) before she was even of school age. His death was devastating to her mother, who struggled to bring home food and ensure that her family had a safe place to live. Her mother worked the street, selling her body for food. Marja did not get the care she needed, and by the age of four wound up malnourished, with rickets.

Because of the instability at home, Marja was adopted by a fire chief of one of the large cities of Sweden. During her childhood, she remembers staring at a little crucifix that hung on a wall and felt as if someone said to her, *"You'll find God if you go to America."* So when she was old enough, she came to the United

States and accepted Christ in one of my revival meetings when I was a young evangelist. Then we got married just a few months after we met.

You can imagine all the transitions Marja had to master. A new country, different culture, new faith, new language—and married to a young evangelist and pastor affiliated with a very conservative denomination. It was difficult for her to adjust to the lifestyle.

Back then the women in my church were not allowed to wear makeup or draw attention to themselves by wearing fashionable clothes. Marja had actually been a beauty queen in Sweden and was used to presenting herself in a very stylish way, so these restrictive boundaries were hard for her to understand and embrace.

We were young and in love, but these trying circumstances got our marriage off to a rough start. Every night before the church service, we would have "inspection," and I'd tell her, "Please take your makeup off." The dress guidelines put such a stress on our relationship that we decided to suspend itinerant evangelism. At the time my dad was pastoring the church in Kansas City, and I took a position in that ministry. This allowed Marja and me time to adjust to the challenges we were facing.

One day I was getting ready to leave the house to go to work, and Marja was standing at the door with her suitcase in hand. She said, "I'm going to leave. I just can't take this. I'm going to go back to San Francisco to stay with some friends."

I was heartbroken and begged her not to go. She wouldn't change her mind, though, so I drove her to the airport. She got on the plane and flew to Northern California. I was dazed and emotionally deflated. All day long I kept thinking my life was a wreck and my ministry was over. A divorced pastor? There was no such thing in our churches in those days.

After dragging myself through my duties that day, I returned home and tried to sleep. You can imagine how fruitless that exercise was. While I was tossing and turning, the phone rang. It was Marja calling from San Francisco: "You know, I think I made a terrible mistake. Can I come back?"

Of course I said yes, and the next day I returned to the airport to get her.

Once we reached the parking lot, even before we got in the car, we had a talk about our future together and sealed it with a prayer. In that prayer we made a commitment to God: "Lord, we're going to make this work, for better or worse, for richer or poorer, in sickness and in health. With Your help we will make this marriage work."

Here we are, more than fifty years later, still married, still in love, still ministering together in our unique ways with three children serving God and pastoring great churches. That half-hour conversation in the parking lot at the airport was a game changer.

TIME FOR EACH OTHER

A common challenge pastors face is that some members of their church expect them to be available 24/7. I've told my congregation that I am always accessible, but after 5:00 p.m., when I go home, it is best to leave me alone except in emergencies. They have a choice to make: to have a pastor who is their buddy or a pastor who is a man of God. If I'm going to be a man of God, I've got to spend time with God, my wife, and my family.

Over a lifetime of ministry, Marja and I have had to learn how to protect time for each other. There are times when the cell phones have to be turned off and other distractions minimized.

> If I'm going to be a man of God, I've got to
> spend time with God, my wife, and my family.

I really like how my assistant, Lynn Lane, and her husband, Dale, preserve a special time to recharge as a couple. They both have demanding jobs that pull them in different directions each day. When they finish a day of work they're dog-tired, and by the end of a week they're wiped out. Because they work at the church, their days off are Friday and Saturday. They've developed a routine that helps restore their individual and joint mental and physical energy. Lynn described how it works:

Our weekend starts on Friday, so Dale and I like to start the day off by going to Starbucks. For the first thirty minutes, we just sit there. We don't talk to each other, we drink our coffee, we read the paper, and we watch the people around us... That initial thirty minutes of being together [before we start talking] is still very important for our marriage. I let him have his space because he needs it after a rough week. In the same way, he lets me have my space. We have lots of things that we are interested in together, and yet we have some separate interests too. But that half hour to start off our days of rest is very important to us.

What wisdom there is in making sure that our marriages receive attention on a regular basis—even if the time commitment starts with just a half hour!

23

BUILD A HEALTHY FAMILY

Half-Hour Power Principle:
Children need a large quantity of quality time.

S trangely, one of the greatest causes of stress in American life is the family. Even though—or perhaps because—these are the people we love, our relationships with family members cause all types of expectations, anxieties, fears, pressure, disappointment, frustration, and confusion.

The challenges of family life have been heavily researched, well documented, expansively analyzed, widely commented on, and the subject of countless programs and proposed solutions. One of the few things most of those involved in this arena seem to agree on is that family relationships all benefit from the investment of more time. Even thirty minutes can make a big difference!

Family relationships all benefit
from the investment of more time.

If the family is a collection of people related by blood, marriage, or adoption, who share space and experiences, and who are most capable of generating trust and understanding in the process of supporting each other, then why is the family such a source of stress? I suppose an entire book could be devoted to an-swering that question—describing life stages, developmental needs, generational differences, cultural influences, interpersonal dynamics, and so on. The bottom line for me is that the family consists of people, and all human beings are unique and, therefore, challenging. If you struggle to have a healthy and pleasant family experience, you're normal. But if you use some half hours wisely, your family life can be more fulfilling and productive.

I always sigh in frustration when people say how much easier it must be to be a pastor or in a pastor's family—you know, because we only work on Sun-days, the church pays for our housing, everyone respects the pastor's family, and so forth. In my experience, having grown up as a pastor's son as well as serving as a pastor for decades, none of those ideas is tethered to reality. If anything, it seems that the opposite is true.

Studies have shown that the average senior pastor works sixty to seventy hours each week; their marriages are more stressful than most because of the de-mands placed on their time and emotions; their children struggle in the fishbowl of pastoral life; and it is often more difficult to develop friendships because you have to be so guarded and careful in what you say.

Despite this, I experimented with some approaches that seemed to work well for our family. One of those tactics was to zealously guard our family time. It's often a difficult paradox for pastors—as it is with many executives and working people—that those who rely on the leader also want that leader to have a stable and renewing family life. You can't have it both ways, so you have to make your decision of what matters more and follow through on that choice.

The choice I made—and which I have never regretted—was to work as hard and smart as I could during working hours and then to fully devote myself to my family during our prescribed family hours. Some people in the congrega-tion occasionally were frustrated by my inaccessibility when they wanted me on nights or weekends, but you cannot please everybody all of the time. You make the best choices you can and live with the consequences.

BE PRESENT AND A GOOD LISTENER

One of the best skills you can develop that will help build up your family is the ability to listen. We live in a communicative society; we spend hours on our mobile phones or other devices, telling people what we believe they need to know or just passing the time in conversation. But an equally valuable skill is to know how to listen to what is being said—directly or indirectly.

Over the years I have spent a lot of time driving. When our children were young, I discovered that time spent in the car could produce some tangible and valuable results. My boys, especially, treated those times as a prize to be treasured because they knew they had Dad's undivided attention. Rather than making mobile calls or trying to catch up on the news via radio or even seeking a few minutes of relaxation by listening to music, having a purposeful exchange with family members while driving can be a consistently fruitful exercise.

I'll never forget my first pastorate in Davenport, Iowa. Members of the congregation donated their time to construct every building on the campus. It took us about eight years, but it was the only way we could afford to expand our facilities so we could help more people. Almost every free night for those eight years, I spent time helping our construction teams build those four structures. If you know what the winters are like in Iowa, then you know how frigid and raw it gets. Working outside in that weather for three or four hours a night really takes the starch out of you.

Because I usually put in my construction time after dinner, sometimes my sons would ask if they could come with me to the church grounds. They were too young to be of much help, it was a bit dangerous on the construction site for youngsters, and I really could not focus on them during that time. But sometimes they were insistent and came up with good solutions, like playing in the gym while waiting for me to finish.

One night when they asked to accompany me, I told them, "Boys, the only time I would be able to spend with you would be when we're in the car driving there and then driving home. That's not much."

Their response stopped me: "Yeah, but, Dad, we'll get to be with you." So we drove the half hour to the church grounds and later that night reversed it. I was very attentive to them during the drive time because I realized for them it was not just getting out of the house or hanging out at church with their friends or maybe getting to go to bed a little later than usual. To them, simply spending time in my presence was meaningful.

Another time we had a board meeting at the church building. Once again, the boys had begged to join me and I relented. That night the board meeting went rather late, and when I emerged from the meeting, I nearly tripped over them. They had fallen asleep on the floor next to the boardroom door, using choir robes as blankets. So I carried them out to the car, still asleep, and laid Matthew gently across the backseat, buckled him in, and put Luke in the front seat. He wiggled around a bit and then put his head on my leg while we drove home. I carried them into the house and tucked them into bed.

As I was leaving Luke's room, his eyes squinted open and he softly said, "Dad, thank you for taking me with you. I'd rather be with you than anybody in all the world."

That really touched my heart, so I went back, sat on the edge of the bed, and tried to explain my thinking to him. "Luke, I want you to know that the reason I spend so much time working and returning to the church every night is not because I don't love you. I want you to be able to grow up in this country like I did. It's free. And we play ball and enjoy the freedom and all the things I've enjoyed. The hope for keeping our country strong is having a strong church throughout America. That's why I go. And I want you to know I love you."

We talked for a few more minutes, ended our time with a prayer, and then he turned over and went back to sleep. That was one of the most precious half hours I can remember. It was a simple but powerful time—the kind of time you can have with your family members too. It comes from being fully present with those loved ones and listening carefully to what they say and what it means. That's one of the keys to building a great family. Today Luke is the lead pastor of Phoenix First Assembly.

DREAMING TOGETHER

Here's an example of a thirty-minute activity I did with our family almost every week when the kids were young.

Every Monday night we went out to dinner at a restaurant. During those evenings we would set aside time to discuss and plan our family's next summer vacation. We took it seriously. We would get out maps, travel guides, newspaper articles—whatever we could lay our hands on to help us think through our upcoming adventure. We would get so excited that we could hardly wait to take the trip.

As you might guess, we usually had a lot more fun imagining the vacation and planning it than we actually experienced on those journeys. It was rare when the vacation actually lived up to the pretrip hype and expectations.

As we all look back on those experiences now, we agree that the half hours spent every Monday night envisioning our idyllic vacations were some of our greatest times together. Today we realize that the trips were not as important as the year we spent bonding through the weekly exchanges.

Our children are in their thirties and forties now, but we remain a tight-knit group. I firmly believe that's because of the choice I made to prioritize our time together, every day, and to devote my half hours to them collectively and individually during those times.

Every night we ate dinner together. As the kids grew, we'd attend sports practices or games but would return home and reunite around ice cream or conversation. Again, those were half-hour blocks that I could have spent crafting my next sermon or preparing for upcoming meetings, but my priority was to build up my family, so those other options had to take the back burner. Every night we would get back together and enjoy each other's company, whether the featured activity was telling jokes, discussing world events, wrestling, or some other shared activity.

For the record, in more than a half-century of ministry, I've come to believe that when we argue about whether a family needs quality time or quantity time, we are missing the point. It's not an either-or question. Your family—your spouse and your children—require both the best time you can give them and as much time as you can give them. Please do not misunderstand the point of this chapter. I'm not saying give your family a half hour and consider your family investment done. Instead, look for those extra half hours that you can devote to them that represent quality time while increasing the quantity of time shared with them.

24

RAISE KIDS RIGHT

Half-Hour Power Principle:
Build character in children by showing them yours.

C an you really have a tremendous impact on a child in just thirty minutes? Oh, *for sure!*

If your kids give you thirty minutes, take it!

I know that some parents think the idea of planning half-hour activities with their kids is strange. But something else I discovered is that kids get bored quickly. They may enjoy thirty minutes of family banter, but then they get squirrelly and want to do something different. You cannot take that personally; that's just how kids are, especially in this era of electronic distractions and 24/7 entertainment.

If your kids give you thirty minutes, take it! You can throw a lot of baseballs or footballs to your son in a half hour. You can work through a significant relational problem that has been plaguing your daughter all day—in a half hour. You can give them guidance on their homework in a half hour. You can dream about their future together in thirty minutes. You can even buy your daughter a dress in a half hour—at least once! Those half hours I spent shopping with Kristie really paid dividends. She is one of the great leaders in our church.

The options are endless, but their attention span isn't. Once you realize that they're losing their focus or interest, it's okay to move on. Maybe they need some space to reflect on what you just said, or they know they have to balance family time with their own to-do list. Be grateful for the chance to spend the half hour with them, and be available for the next opening they offer.

Essentially what you're doing in those times together is deepening and strengthening your relationship. At the end of the day, that's really all you have that matters in life. And because families are the cornerstone of the church, what better investment could you make than devoting yourself to the needs of your family?

CHARACTER DEVELOPMENT

One of the biggest responsibilities that parents have is developing the character of their children.

There are all kinds of strategies for doing so. I found that one of the most effective was taking a half hour to focus on a particular character trait and help my kids to own that attribute.

The Bible alludes to at least four dozen different character traits. None is necessarily more important than any other. It is valuable for these characteristics to be in a parent's mind so that when an incident occurs that opens a door for a teaching moment, you can be aware of that opportunity and ready to boldly pounce on it.

Here are some of the most significant character traits to be developed:

- Compassion
- Consistency
- Discipline
- Encouragement
- Gentleness
- Honesty
- Humility
- Joy

- Justice
- Kindness
- Love
- Loyalty
- Maturity
- Mercy
- Patience
- Perseverance
- Reliability
- Self-Control
- Sincerity
- Stability
- Trustworthiness

If you're a parent like me, you can look at each of these traits and recall at least one experience with your kids when you had a great teaching moment regarding that trait. Sometimes I could not explore the opportunity with them in real time; I had to return to it later, when my schedule allowed. But having those half-hour encounters related to experiences that were very real to the children was a mighty teaching tool.

LIFE LESSONS IN THIRTY MINUTES

Even when you're having fun together as a family, you can use those times to drive home life lessons. If something would come up in our joking or conversations that was a bit sensitive or controversial, my wife and I never backed away from the discussion; we viewed it as a teaching moment. We didn't keep things hidden from the kids, separating adult issues from what we thought was youth appropriate. I believe that is one reason why our children never got bitter toward us; they knew we were honest with them and that we would address the things that were on their minds.

Some of our half-hour conversations began as a simple response to something they'd heard whispers about, some kind of dissension in our church or perhaps a disagreement I'd had with another church leader. We would talk about the matter, but my point was not to convert them to my way of thinking, but rather for them to learn how the world works. It enabled them to feel as if they were engaged in ministry with me because we considered the options and made decisions together (although I had the final word).

I'd lift a life lesson from each situation we discussed. My style was to come up with a short and simple statement that they can remember to capture the spirit of the lesson. Some of the lessons we discussed included:

"When you stop dreaming, you stop living."

"Everybody has needs, so find a need and fill it."

"To live life to the fullest, enlarge your circle of love."

These big-picture ideas, which I wanted to plant in their minds, came naturally during discussions we'd have on the spur of the moment. Rather than run to my study and compose a few pages for my next book, my commitment was to build up my family during those sacred times together each night.

FAMILY DEVOTIONS?

Many people seem surprised to learn that in our home, we have never had family devotions. By now you understand how seriously I take the Bible and how dependent I am on God's Word for guidance and hope. I prayed that all of my children would be used by God in meaningful service to His will and His kingdom. But my kids were at the church building, for services and events, four or five times a week. I observed people during those times and noticed that a lot of the families that had devotions together and spent loads of time at the church lived like the devil during the rest of the week. It seemed clear to me that while devotions are not bad, they aren't the cure-all either.

So my philosophy is that you use life experiences as your devotions. Every time something happened that we could learn a lesson from, we would talk about it and try to figure out if there was insight to be gleaned from that incident. I began the practice of making a mental note of such experiences and carving out a half hour for us to talk about them.

My kids realized that this was how Dad was going to teach them God's principles, through our daily conversations about events that occurred in our midst. Those "devotionals" could happen at any moment, at any time during the day, once or several times each day. It became a natural thing for us, and we did not feel embarrassed that we did not have a traditional type of devotional time.

In hindsight, with all of our children now grown, in love with God, engaged in full-time ministry, and experiencing a wonderful family life of their own, I feel that the approach served us well.

You can certainly bless your kids in a half hour. The only question is how you choose to do it. *It all starts with your determination to make sure that you do it.*

TAKING RESPONSIBILITY

One of the toughest things for children to understand and accept is responsibility. It takes a series of focused encounters—half hours—not only to effectively get across the concept but also to instill the desire to accept responsibility for one's behavior.

To drive home that point, I told the kids a lot of stories. One that they loved was when I explained that if I were driving a hundred miles per hour down the highway and someone hit my car from the rear, it's my fault for going too slow! They loved that. It was goofy and a little irrational, but it caught their attention and made the point: take responsibility for what happens in your life. Don't put the blame on others.

We had a lot of great half-hour talks about that!

FAMILY AND MEDIA

You know who probably understands the power of a half hour as well as anybody? The media—especially television networks. They program a lot of their content in half-hour modules. Based on lots of research about the impact of the media on our lives, we can document the powerful grip the media has on the minds and hearts of Americans—and not always for the better.

Researcher George Barna has written about the dramatic influence that the media has on what we think and do—more influence than anything else in our lives—especially among our children. Barna's research indicates that media use has literally become an addiction for a majority of Americans.[18]

One way to combat a half hour of media effect on your kids is to spend some time with them discussing their media use and the substance of the content to which they're exposing themselves. The life-lesson approach that we took with our children extended into the area of media choices, with outstanding results.

The music young people listen to is not always in their best interests. When my kids were growing, certain types of rock music were the big thing. I never forbade them to listen to such music, though I did discourage it. We had a pivotal discussion about it, and I let them choose the path to follow.

I opened our discussion by establishing my perspective: "Why would you want to listen to that music?" I asked them. "I know your friends are listening to it and you want to fit in, but if you listen carefully, you'll find that the views they teach in their music are not the views that we hold, are they?"

They mulled that over, and we exchanged a few more thoughts about the song lyrics, the lifestyles of the musicians, the impact of music on who you become, and the like. One of the kids asked if I was going to forbid them to listen to these musicians.

"Well, here's the situation," I explained. "When you leave this house to go to school or visit a friend, you would be able to listen to that music. I wouldn't know about it. I couldn't stop you. It's your choice of what you want to put into your head and heart. Personally, I don't think it's too smart. My advice to you is don't do it."

And I left it at that. No threats, no yelling, no guilt trips, no emotional meltdown, no manipulation. A polite, low-key conversation during a thirty-minute break gave them plenty to think about without the emotional or spiritual baggage that sometimes clouds such decisions.

In the end, they talked some more among themselves, and then I never heard about it again. They decided they did not need to listen to that music and that the absence of it in their lives wouldn't be a big deal.

Not too long afterward we had a similar dialogue about movies. In our church tradition in the past, you did not go to see movies in a theater. Egged on by their classmates, the kids thought that was pretty old-fashioned and silly. I personally did not have a big concern about the concept of movies and told them that there is nothing morally wrong with watching a good movie. After all, they would regularly watch movies on television, so what was the difference? But I wanted to be consistent in the lessons I taught them and added that because I was the pastor of a church in a denomination whose doctrine taught that seeing movies in a theater was inappropriate, my life would be a lot easier and less stressful if they did not go to the theater.

Once again, after our discussion about why people make such a big deal about this, how the church's position came about, what their friends would say, and so forth, they quietly and uneventfully bucked the cultural trend and decided against going to the movie theater.

Long afterward I asked them about those choices and discovered that they trusted me enough to take my advice. That trust was built over a lifetime of similar conversations during our half hours, reinforced by my modeling the choices I recommended to them. We had a strong relationship based on including each other in the guts of our lives and spending time together studying life lessons.

25

PEOPLE ARE JUST PEOPLE

Half-Hour Power Principle:
Life is hard—we must help each other.

I learned something important about loving others from my dad. He often would say, "People are just people—we're all a mess, Christian or otherwise."

All people fail, but Jesus never fails.

We do have to accept people for who they are and find those who are willing to grow, and then we can do our best to help them. Those people who are struggling are a gift from God, because we are able to pour our lives into them.

In the process, we have to remember that all people fail, but Jesus never fails, so we have to keep our eyes on Him. If we don't, then we fail the people whom we could have blessed—and that's our fault, not theirs.

HELPING THE HURTING

When my kids were in school, I used to try to attend all of their sports events. One day I was at a football game in which my son Matthew was playing. At one point the referee made a terrible call. It was obvious to everyone in the stands how wrong the call was. There was the usual blast of boos and shouts of frustration. But what really stood out was one father who was beside himself and totally went off—I mean, he went completely berserk.

He was so far over the top that the referees conferred with each other and actually penalized our team again because of this guy's outrageous behavior. They told him to stop the harassment, but that just fueled his fire and he kept at it. So they slapped a second penalty against our team, and after he kept going, they leveled a third penalty against us. By the time they were done, the ball had been moved halfway down the field, just a few yards from our end zone, putting us in a really bad situation.

At this point, everyone in the stadium was on this guy's case, but he kept ranting and raving; he'd just lost it. Finally, they had him removed from the stands, and then the game continued. I cannot imagine how his son felt, watching that horror show unfold with his dad at the center of attention.

This father must have cooled off as he was exiting the stands. He went to a far corner of the field and sat in an out-of-the-way seat. I watched him take that long walk and then noticed his shoulders rising and falling after he got to his outcast location. You could tell he was sobbing. Something had to be done, so I walked over, sat down beside him, and softly spoke to him.

"Buddy, that was a terrible call, no doubt about it. It was awful," I said. "They probably deserved that tirade."

His cheeks were wet as he stared at the ground and whispered, "I'm so embarrassed. I made a fool of myself. Nobody will like me or accept me after that outburst."

There was a lot of truth in his observation, but that wasn't the kind of "encouragement" he needed. "You know what?" I began. "You're a good man. I know you. You love your boy. You're at every one of his practices." I knew that was true because I was also at every one of the practices, and this guy was there every time. "Listen to me," I said more forcefully, looking him in the eye. "Be encouraged. Don't let this destroy you. Come on back to the stands with me. Everybody understands."

My speech didn't get him to jump up and enthusiastically rush back to his seat. Instead, he leaned over, let his head fall on my shoulder, and cried for a few minutes. But once he pulled himself together, we took a slow walk back to where the rest of the parents were sitting. He learned a lesson. People were nice to him, even after his fit of anger. I didn't have any magic words; I merely saw a person in pain who needed some encouragement. That guy knew he had made a big mistake; he needed someone to tell him that despite that error he was still loved and lovable.

KIND WORDS

Countless times I've been the recipient of kind words that have lifted my failing spirits. So here are a few examples of words of affirmation that anyone can speak—and quite often. Thank the people you know for what they have done for you. If as a grown child you tell an aging parent how much you realize the parent had to sacrifice for your best interests and how much you appreciate the love and encouragement Mom or Dad has given over the years, that's a big deal. When you send a little handwritten note to a friend expressing your love and gratitude to him or her, that's truly special. When you write an e-mail to your child's coach or teacher or youth leader and express your thanks, and mention the positive changes you've seen in your child as a result of that person's efforts, you've touched someone's heart for the better.

Take a look at all of the lives that nourish you during the day; let those people know what it means to you. It will certainly mean a lot to them.

Part 7

The Power of a Half Hour to

CHANGE THE WORLD

26

SERVE IN A LOVING CHURCH

Half-Hour Power Principle:
Help make your church relevant.

Yes, I'm a pastor, so I know it's expected that I will say something like this, but I mean it with all my heart: *I love the local church!* And the main reason is that when we function together as a body the way Jesus asked us to do it, we become a powerful force to "find a need and fill it."

Find a need and fill it.

People have a lot of ideas these days about what the church should or should not be doing to minister to the needs of individual Christians as well as be relevant to the world. But after many decades of serving as a pastor, as well as growing up in a pastor's family, I am convinced that the basic vision for a healthy church has not changed. This is how a church is relevant: if it tells people the good news of the gospel (brings souls to Christ) and ministers to people who have needs. And this sharing the gospel and helping people is the challenge for every person in the church, not just the pastor and staff. All of us can find ways to help build the Lord's church using half hours intentionally.

I have frequently been asked over the years what my "secret" is to seeing a church grow. There is no secret—just God's plan. I've also been asked if I think there is anything wrong with a small church. I do have a favorite answer for that one: "No, if it only stays small for a week!" For if you have a New Testament church, you *cannot stay small.* In the book of Acts, we see how people were added daily to the church (see 2:47). That says to me that in seven days, then, a small church will be getting bigger!

In saying that, I know full well that it takes a combination of a leader's vision, acceptance of that vision by the people, and movement of the Holy Spirit to make things happen in any church—small or large. Not long after I began to serve as pastor of Phoenix First Assembly Church, I challenged the people to do four things for a month: pray every day, fast one day a week and ask God to send a revival, bring an unsaved person with them every Sunday morning, and tithe for a month.

After that month a fresh anointing fell on me and on the church. At every service people came forward to be saved. And the number of ministries to help the down and hurting in our city grew almost on a weekly basis. And most of these outreaches were started by "ordinary" members of the church who felt called to help others.

This is where you come in! I urge you to get involved in a significant way in the church you attend. Find people to help—inside or outside the walls of your church—and start helping them. Tell them that God loves them and Jesus died for them—then invite them to be saved. And, of course, minister to their needs along the way. And if the church you attend is not interested in this kind of activity, then prayerfully consider finding another church that is.

WHOLE BODY SERVICE

I can hardly sit still when I think of the incredible blessings that come and the excitement that bursts forth when a church catches a vision for seeing the lost saved and helped.

As a pastor, one of my jobs is to help people express love and grace toward others. So, for instance, every year our church gives Christmas presents to thousands of poor children in our city who otherwise would not get anything for Christmas. We have the people of our congregation buy the gifts and bring them to the church, wrapped and ready to give. Honestly, it would be a lot easier to simply take a special offering and buy the gifts en masse and distribute them. But that would not give people the same experience of expressing the kind of love that is involved in actually thinking about what gift to get, buying it, wrapping it, and giving it to a needy child.

It's the same way at Thanksgiving, when we give away thousands of turkeys to low-income families. Again, the church could order a few truckloads of turkeys and get them delivered to our parking lot. But the joy of giving—and the marvel of receiving a gift from someone who cared enough to pick it out, pay for it, box it up, and personally deliver it—would be absent.

It doesn't take a genius to buy, wrap, and present a gift. But these expressions of care and compassion can make a big difference in someone's life. It might be the best investment of thirty minutes you experience all week.

The idea of the body of Christ pulling together is what really got the Dream Center in Los Angeles off the ground. When the church began, my son Matthew called me to say how much he believed that at Thanksgiving the Dream Center should give a turkey to each household in the adjoining neighborhood to demonstrate how much we love and care for those people. I went to my congregation in Phoenix and asked each family to donate a turkey that we would then ship to Los Angeles.

Sure enough, we received more than three thousand turkeys for the Dream Center to give away! Just before we put them in the refrigerated truck to send to Los Angeles, Matthew called me up and said he had discovered that the Hispanic families living there preferred chickens to turkeys. I laughed and told Matthew, "Sorry, son, it's too late to change now. Just tell them these are chickens on steroids."

Matthew and his team distributed the turkeys, and people in that area were surprised and ecstatic. We talked with each other about the fact that we had no formal training in cross-cultural ministry but that love transcends all cultural boundaries and language barriers.

How I love the way God releases the resources He has stored in the body of Christ!

That success led Matthew to take things a step further. Shortly after Thanksgiving he called me and said he needed Christmas presents for the neighborhood kids, most of whom were too poor to expect anything at Christmas. When I asked how many he was thinking about, he said ten thousand presents should fill the need. Ten thousand gifts, wrapped, age appropriate, shipped from Phoenix to Los Angeles!

Once again I asked my congregation to be generous, and they outdid themselves, giving well over the ten thousand gifts for the LA community, plus thousands more for the poor in Phoenix! One fellow in our congregation was so inspired that he personally donated five thousand new bicycles. When all of those magnificent gifts were distributed to the children in the poor families around the church, they knew one thing for sure: they were not merely receiving a bunch of unexpected presents, but they were truly loved by the people from the church. The church folks had provided very tangible expressions of their love to people they had never even met—all for the sake of Christ.

To show that its ministry was not just about seasonal giveaways, the Dream Center then installed a weight room for the neighborhood people to use, followed by pouring concrete and installing hoops for the nearby youth to play basketball. These were not simply church-growth techniques; the purpose was to show these people that we loved them and wanted them to experience the best that God has for them in life.

Thankfully, the Dream Center got a reputation for caring about the people, and it began to grow like a weed. The other outreach programs at the church saw a substantial increase in participation as the neighborhood people trusted the church more and more. Attendance grew steadily, and altar calls were getting two to three hundred people accepting Jesus Christ as their Savior.

Love was the "secret" ingredient.

Be Creative in Finding Needs to Fill

Former foster-care children are one of the most ignored groups of people in our society. A large number of these young people have not earned a high-school diploma or a GED, they no longer have a safe environment to live in, and they have no family to turn to for help. All of a sudden they're thrown into the world, expected to make it on their own. They celebrate their eighteenth birthday, and before they know it, the social worker shows up with a plastic trash bag for their belongings and officially removes them from the program. Many of them wind up on skid row or being exploited on the streets.

Our church in Phoenix, as well as the Dream Center in Los Angeles, saw this tragedy and became deeply immersed in helping former foster-care children. At Easter, my son Luke asked the people in our congregation to take a suitcase or duffel bag and fill it with all the things that a child would need at age eighteen. Hundreds of families brought in suitcases filled with the possessions they felt an eighteen-year-old would need: clothing, toiletries, underwear, accessories, shoes, you name it. Every year now on Easter Sunday, the building is crammed with hundreds of suitcases; it looks like a room full of people waiting to board a cruise ship.

Now, when social workers go to tell foster children that it is time for them to leave the program, we accompany them and bring along those filled suitcases. We give them to the young people, along with an invitation to stay at the Dream Center if they need housing, an opportunity to get a GED through our program, the possibility of entering our job-training program, and an invitation to join us at the church if they'd like to do so.

Our people have a special place in their hearts for foster children, and they enjoy expressing God's love to them by spending a half hour shopping to fill a suitcase that can help a desperate young person survive after the government support ends.

By the way, I cannot count how many of those young people have told me and other staff members how much those gifts meant to them. They had dreaded being turned out of their foster homes but found that the suitcases packed with necessities meant that somebody understood their plight and cared about them.

Oh, how I love the *relevant,* local church—being the very body of the Lord Jesus in action!

27

SPREAD THE GOSPEL

Half-Hour Power Principle:
Take opportunities to share God's love.

I think God gives us divine appointments every day of our lives. Sometimes we keep those appointments; sometimes we don't. Every day you have encounters with all kinds of people—at work, in the grocery store or shopping mall, in the neighborhood, at your child's school, in the doctor's office—everywhere. Each of these encounters is an opportunity for you to help someone get right with God.

How important are these short opportunities? The director of our Dream Center in Phoenix, Brian Steele, knows exactly how significant they are. Brian came to Phoenix and became the director of outreach ministries for a parachurch group. This organization was doing terrific work with the poor and needy, and Brian was flourishing there.

. God gives us divine appointments every day.

He recalls a turning point in his life, though, while giving food and clothing to homeless people. Part of the organization's philosophy was that they were going to do good works for the sake of Jesus but not tell the recipients about Jesus. Brian got to know the homeless people quickly, seeing them return week after week. What got to him, though, was one particular homeless lady who disappeared without notice.

"There was one lady who had been coming consistently," Brian recalled. "She was probably in her forties but very hardened; she had clearly been on the streets for quite a while. One day I was serving food, and I didn't see her there. It didn't make much of an impression on me; I was just aware of her absence. Then the next week she was missing again, and then the next as well.

"I started asking a couple of the other folks who always served, and they said that she had died of a heroin overdose a few weeks earlier. I was stunned. I felt so convicted that here I had been, passing out beans and burritos, giving her and all the others the bread of this world, but at no point did I ever touch base with her about the love of Christ or explain to her how much God loved her.

"I spent the last half hour of that shift thinking deeply about the purpose of my life and what it means to be called to the mission field. Is it just about giving food and clothing? That was a real change moment in my life. From that point on, I have been determined to not only address the physical needs of the poor but to also be about my Father's business of telling people about the true bread of life."

I fully understand Brian's heartbreak. As followers of Jesus we are commanded to share the good news of our salvation with others. If we are willing, He will give us the opportunities—those divine appointments.

A DESERT ENCOUNTER

A great example of this came at the least-expected moment for me. First some background...

When I was in school, I was a long-distance runner. I had a dream of someday running from Los Angeles to New York City, stopping to preach in the big cities along the way. My plan was to use the running to generate media interest and draw a crowd to preach to. But after I finished school, things got busy with full-time ministry, marriage and children, and other obligations, so it never happened. But on my sixtieth birthday, I decided to make at least part of that dream a reality, so I made plans to run from Phoenix to LA as a way to raise money for the Dream Center.

I started running on October 4, 1997, and finished in nineteen days—not exactly a world-record pace, but I averaged about a marathon a day and ran a total of 436 miles across the Mojave Desert in a pretty taxing climate.

A couple of days after leaving Phoenix and about sixty miles into the trip, I was moving steadily toward Los Angeles. Throughout my run, I was trailed in a car by my assistant Gary. You're not allowed to run on the freeways, so I had to take back roads.

At that point, I was running down a road that had once been the highway, but they had chopped up the asphalt and made it a dirt road again. Gary had to return to Phoenix to pick up something we'd forgotten, so for a while I was out there by myself. It wasn't scary; there was nobody on the road, which is near an Indian reservation. I was deep in thought while chugging down the road, when suddenly a red pickup truck stopped a little ways ahead of me. The guy behind the wheel just sat there and watched me. I kept going, wondering what he was doing. That was when I did start to wonder about my safety.

I went a ways past where he had parked, and then suddenly he started up his truck and started following me. Now I got nervous. Then he pulled up beside me and called out, "Where are you going?"

"Los Angeles," I yelled back.

He looked at me and asked, "What for?"

Still running, I yelled back, "I'm raising money for a place out there called the Dream Center. It's a place where people can come and dream again, people who have an alcoholic problem or drug problem, any kind of addiction or big problem, or if they just got out of prison."

The truck continued next to me for a little while before he turned his head back toward me. When he did, I could see tears in his eyes and he yelled back, softer than before, "You know, that sounds like a place I need to be." He was a Native American fellow and seemed pretty ruggedly built. "They call me the Michael Jordan of the Indians because I'm a great basketball player. I play in tournaments all over. But now I'm looking at prison because of my drug habit."

He kept pace with me for a few more minutes, and then I saw Gary pull up behind us.

I put my finger up to signal the guy in the red truck to hold on a minute, then I jogged back to Gary's car. "I'm really glad you're back, Gary. This man needs to talk to you," I said and then winked at him. He knew what I meant. I turned back to the Native American man and said, "If you have a few minutes, I'd like you to talk to my friend Gary. We work together at the Dream Center, and I believe he can help you."

Gary and the man started talking with each other, and I moved down the road, continuing my trek toward Los Angeles. Every minute or so, I turned around to see if they were still talking. The man was sitting in his red truck, and Gary was standing outside of it, talking away. After a while I could just barely see a little speck in the distance.

Eventually Gary drove up in his car and pulled alongside of me. "Our brother just accepted Christ as his personal Savior," he reported, a big grin on his face. "And then he asked if I could baptize him. I told him, 'There's no water here.' But the guy kept insisting, 'But I want to get baptized.' I kept saying, 'Can't you see we're in the desert? There's no water anywhere around here.' But he didn't care; he was determined that he was going to get baptized."

I smiled as I kept running. I love stories like this.

Gary continued, "So I had an idea and went to the trunk of the car and found a big bottle of Evian water. I walked back to his truck and told him to stick his head out the window. He looked at me kinda funny, but he did it, and I started pouring water over his head while saying the prayer for him. He asked if that really was a baptism, and I told him, 'That'll do until we get back to Phoenix.'"

Shortly after that, the man did go to prison, as he expected, but as soon as he was released, he visited our church, and we baptized him in front of thousands of people, including his wife and son. They were all beaming afterward. That decision not only changed his life forever but probably saved his family too.

It all came from that thirty-minute tag-team exchange he had with Gary and me in the middle of the desert while I was running to LA. God can do the things you would never expect if you're open to being used when He so chooses.

Do you know someone who is living his or her life without Christ at the center, without the grace that makes real life possible? It doesn't take long to lead somebody to the Lord. It takes a real dialogue about purpose, sin, Jesus Christ, forgiveness, and restoration. But what could be more life-changing or more life-giving than bringing someone to the foot of the Cross and helping that person to know the love and mercy of our Father in heaven?

Within thirty minutes, you can empower someone to make the most important decision in his or her life.

28

GIVE EXTRAVAGANTLY

Half-Hour Power Principle:
Practice giving until you get really good at it.

When I was a young boy, I read a very short book, *Try Giving Yourself Away* by David Dunn. The book was about a man who spent his life giving ideas to people. He'd go to a restaurant and give ideas on how the owners could improve their restaurant. He'd go to businesses and offer ideas on how they could improve their business. He never charged for his ideas. Even though he gave his time away, he became a wealthy man.

It took me about a half hour to read, but that book left a lifelong impression on me. I was captivated by the thought of giving my life away. It is so consistent with how Jesus lived and ministered. I've been practicing that principle ever since.

> The value of the gifts is in what
> the act of giving communicates.

Bestowing love on somebody through the giving of gifts is not about supplying prized possessions. The value of the gifts is in what the act of giving communicates—that the person is being thought about, is cared for, is important enough to justify the effort and resources to get a gift. People appreciate being remembered and getting things that are meaningful to them, regardless of the monetary value. They are seeking indications that they matter and are on your mind and in your heart.

It may be relatively easy to buy a gift for someone that means a lot to that person. I've found that if you give people the gift of your best thinking—like helping them to solve a difficult problem, to develop a creative concept, to refine a plan, or provide some similarly unusual form of assistance—it is appreciated just as much as a material possession would be.

GIVING BACK TO A SAINT

On the ninetieth birthday of the well-known evangelist Oral Roberts, a group of his supporters wanted to honor him for his life's work in ministry. They contacted my son and me at the Dream Center in Los Angeles. As we pondered what we might be able to do to honor Oral, I began to recall all the wonderful things he had done during his lifetime. He is well known for preaching about the concept of seed faith, which helped thousands of churches more effectively teach stewardship and raise money for ministry. He started Oral Roberts University, where thousands of young people have received a terrific education. For years he had a hospital where many people were healed and nursed back to health. He had even awarded me an honorary doctorate some years ago. I respected Oral as a man of God and was thankful for his commitment to being used to bless people and serve God.

Matthew and I discussed the opportunity and agreed that Oral deserved to be shown some love by his spiritual family. So the Dream Center agreed to do something for him at one of its services.

When the day came, he arrived at the church and shuffled down the center aisle, aided by a walker. We seated him in the front row and showed a brief video that the church had put together of some ministry highlights from his life. When it was over, we wanted him to stand and receive some applause and maybe say a few words.

Oral was so frail that we thought he might not be able to speak. He couldn't walk up the stairs to get onto the stage, but apparently he was moved by the presentation. He got inspired and stood at the base of the platform. Holding on to his walker, he began to address the crowd. For almost ten minutes he preached about God's love and grace, ending with a stirring altar call, inviting people to be saved. A number of people's lives were changed that day as God once more spoke through Oral to bring them to faith. It turned out to be the last church service at which Oral ever spoke.

During his sixty-plus years in public ministry, Oral spoke to millions of people at crusades, churches, schools, ministry events, and through his television program. Yet he only allowed them to take an offering for him once. The sponsors of that particular event insisted that he allow them to take a love offering for him. He finally gave in and allowed them to do so. It brought in so much money that he was embarrassed and vowed he would never do it again—and to my knowledge, he never did. Before we finished our service honoring him, God touched my heart and I felt inspired to say we were going to receive an offering for Oral. A lot of people did not realize that in his last years, after he retired from public ministry, he had nothing. He lived in a very humble apartment in Southern California. I told our church, "We're going to receive an offering for Oral tonight. He's a man of great faith, and I would like this to be the largest offering that he has ever received."

All of this happened at our Thursday night service, so most of the audience was young people. They didn't know Oral Roberts from the man in the moon. But we received the offering. Before they began counting the money, I told the accountability team, "This is for a man who believes in miracles. May this be the biggest miracle; I'm going to believe for that." After they finished and came to tell us how much had been collected, we were stunned to see that people had generously given him over $60,000! Then we rejoiced for Oral and praised God for moving people to such generosity.

The next day, Matthew drove down to Orange County to Oral's humble apartment to deliver the money to him. When he received it, he cried and kept thanking Matthew and the church. That little half hour in the service that was devoted to honoring him—the legacy video, the chance to invite people to receive Christ as their Savior, that generous offering, the prayer time we had for him—it meant the world to him. He told Matthew how loved and affirmed he had felt that night.

Think about how little effort it might take to impact someone's life for eternity. It doesn't take a genius to buy, wrap, and present a gift to someone. Or to pick up the phone and make a call to check in on a sick friend. But these expressions of care and compassion can make a big difference in that person's life. And it takes only a few minutes. It might be the best investment of thirty minutes you experience all week.

29

TAKE KINGDOM RISKS

Half-Hour Power Principle:
Take a risk for God—what could be safer?

A leading twentieth-century theologian, Paul Tillich recognized the necessity of risk taking when he said, "He who risks and fails can be forgiven. He who never risks and never fails is a failure in his whole being."[19]

Ouch! I never want to be known as someone who always plays it safe!

Having been in leadership positions since my teens, I have a long history of pursuing audacious outcomes meant to advance the kingdom of God. I am adventurous by nature, but I learned early on that the greater the risk you take, the greater the potential benefits you may gain. Often, the benefit of a half hour is in discerning whether or not a risk is justified.

> The greater the risk you take, the greater
> the potential benefits you may gain.

While Phoenix First was growing and blessing people, I frequently had opportunities to minister in Los Angeles, especially since Matthew and I were co-pastoring a church in a ghetto area there.

One day as I was driving through the city to Matthew's church, I drove by the renowned Angelus Temple, and the Spirit of the Lord spoke to me: *"Someday you're going to be pastor of that church."* That made no sense to me since it was a Foursquare Church and I am ordained by the Assemblies of God. Besides, it was a famous church and must have been doing well, even though it was located in what had become a terrible part of Los Angeles.

Fast forward a few years to another one of my visits to Los Angeles. I had read in the *Los Angeles Times* that Angelus Temple had suffered a split. The congregation had dwindled down to barely one hundred people over the years, and the newspaper reported that about seventy-five of them left for a church in Pasadena. That left only about twenty-five people who stayed. Meanwhile, our ministry at the Los Angeles Dream Center, which was only a few blocks away, had been expanding rapidly; we were out of space. So I told Matthew about the demise of Angelus Temple and suggested that we go talk to the Foursquare executives.

We arranged an appointment and entered their building for the meeting. When we convened, I explained that we had a thriving ministry a few blocks from their site that drew seven to eight hundred people each weekend—but without the benefit of an appropriate facility. I told them about our plans to build a sanctuary that would seat fifteen hundred people but that it would not be big enough to meet our needs. Then I dropped the big idea on them—the risky idea: why not join both ministries together, using the Angelus Temple facility to get people saved and then the Dream Center campus to disciple them?

I half expected them to throw us out of their office. After all, denominations typically compete more than cooperate. But I went on to explain that both denominations essentially believe the same things, and that each campus could remain affiliated with its respective denomination. And, if necessary, Matthew could switch over and become a Foursquare pastor to satisfy their requirements. Before ending my recommendation, I added, "It would be a testimony to the whole world that two denominations are not rivals, but they're willing to use their great assets in the inner city for a higher purpose."

To their credit, they continued the conversation. It took a few months for both sides to work through some of the details, but in the end we were able to bind those two ministries together. The Foursquare denomination completely renovated the interior of the Temple, including modifying the seating and installing a terrific sound system. Then, as the church began to grow, there was no longer sufficient parking available—or at least no safe parking—so they built and paid for a seven-story parking garage. We ended up with a state-of-the-art church facility in downtown Los Angeles—all because we scheduled a thirty-minute meeting to cast vision and take a risk on doing something that religious insiders laughed at. To God's glory, this is now one of the biggest Foursquare churches in America.

Sometimes you can use a thirty-minute exchange to go fishing. By that I mean that you throw some bait in the water and see if you can reel anything in. If the Lord puts the opportunity before you and the idea in your mind, pursue it.

RECRUITING A KEY ASSOCIATE

Another example of a risky exercise was my pursuit of Randy Barton. He has been general counsel to the Assemblies of God but was perhaps best known for the amazing job he did as president and CEO of Assemblies of God Financial Services Group (AGFSG), which is an umbrella entity overseeing the investments of the denomination's foundation, retirement funds, and loans. Under his leadership, the investment pool grew greatly.

One day I was on a plane flying back to Los Angeles. I noticed that Randy was on the same flight, so I made my way up to visit with him for a while. As a member of the foundation board, I was well aware of the financial magic Randy had performed. We were trying to raise money for the Dream Center in LA at the time, and I knew Randy would be an invaluable help to us. We chatted for a half hour about the Dream Center and the plans and needs related to its expansion. At the end of the conversation, I asked him to be sure to contact me if he ever decided to leave AGFSG.

As time went on, I forgot all about that conversation—but Randy didn't. A couple of years later he called me and explained that he was retiring from AGFSG and was exploring his options. "I want to do something worthwhile. If you need me, I'd like to come and help you at the Dream Center. I don't need to be paid much." You couldn't ask for a better answer to prayer than that!

Randy joined us and has done a fabulous job. Thanks to his guidance and efforts, we were able to raise $10 million in private funds and another $20 million from a foundation. That day on that airplane trip, I had been tempted to just sit back in my seat and relax, maybe say something to Randy after the plane landed and we waited for our luggage. But I felt prompted to go and talk to him during the flight, even though the chance of his ever working with the Dream Center was a long shot, at best. That was a conversation that truly paid off handsomely.

Take a risk; invest a half hour in something that might generate tremendous returns—or nothing at all. Life, in some respects, is a numbers game, so you have to keep trying until you get what you need.

CHOOSE A RADICAL SOLUTION

Another of my memorable half-hour risks had its beginning in Nashville. The son of Hank Snow, the famous country singer, is a pastor there, and he invited me to speak at his church. Among the people in attendance that day were Johnny Cash and his wife, June. After the service, Johnny came up to me and said, "Reverend, I really enjoyed your message. I want to do some strong thinking on that. I really thank you."

Not too long afterward, Johnny was scheduled to do a concert in Davenport where I was pastoring. I thought it'd be fun to go to the show and maybe have a chance to visit him after the concert. On my way out of the auditorium, I thought I'd go back to see if I could visit with Johnny. So I went backstage, and I could hear Johnny talking behind a heavy stage curtain. When one of the security men asked to see my pass, I said, "Please tell Johnny Cash that Pastor Tommy Barnett is here and would like to talk to him."

A few minutes went by before I heard a booming voice from behind the curtain say, "Send the reverend in."

I was shown backstage by the security man, shook Johnny's hand, and we sat down to have a chat. I'd thought a lot about this moment before going to the concert and was ready to describe my idea.

"Johnny," I began, "I've got a vision. We have a big stadium here in town,

John O'Donnell Stadium, that can hold thirty thousand people if we use the space right. If you'll come and sing and I'll preach, we'll call it the world's greatest Sunday school. I really believe it will be."

He thought for a moment, then smiled and boomed, "Okay, Reverend, I'll do it." He was generous with his time, spending a half hour with me to discuss what we could do at that event. It was a bit audacious of me to impose on him like that, but he was very gracious and accommodating.

When the time came, Johnny showed up as promised. We drew the largest crowd in the history of the city; thirty thousand people showed up in a town of only one hundred thousand at the time. Johnny didn't come alone, either. He brought along June Carter, the Carter Singers, Carl Perkins (the singer of the hit song "Blue Suede Shoes"), as well as his whole caravan, PA system, and all the trucks. His going rate for such a show at the time was $100,000, but he wouldn't take a penny, not even to cover their travel expenses or his hotel bill. He paid for it all. He sang all kinds of songs that day. The people loved it.

When the time came, I preached. We had six thousand people come forward during my altar call. While people streamed toward the front, Johnny came back out and sang, "Come home, come home, it's supper time…" It was an event people will never forget.

A GIFT FOR THE DREAM CENTER

My son Matthew had his own audacious moment recently. The Dream Center in Los Angeles is supported by churches and ministries all over the world. One of the biggest supporters is speaker and author Joyce Meyer. Every year she holds a meeting with the ministries she has donated to or plans to begin supporting. You never know exactly what she is going to ask you.

So Matthew was invited, and I accompanied him to the meeting.

When we got there, Joyce had the representatives of the various ministries she supports tell her team why they should support them for another year, including any plans for the future. When it was his turn, Matthew stood up and explained what the Dream Center had been doing. But with the time ticking away, and sensing that Joyce was looking for something different, he switched his focus. He began to speak about the dream that had been burning in his heart for a while: to build a special section of the Dream Center for the girls who want to escape and recover from human trafficking. When Matthew talks about his passions, he gets very emotional—and persuasive.

When he finished his off-the-cuff presentation, Joyce said, "We need to take a break."

She and her team left the room for a little while. When they returned, she looked at us and said, "We'd like to give Matthew a million dollars to build the floor to help the trafficked girls." Since then, she has continued to support that effort with generous monthly gifts.

I was so thankful that Matthew had the courage to describe his passion for helping those girls. We now have one of the largest programs for transitioning those young women back into society and developing a healthy sense of self-worth and positive relationships.

Matthew's thirty-minute risk paid off.

TAKE A RISK TO HELP SOMEONE

Of course, some risks are bigger than others.

When we started pastoring the church in Phoenix, we were located downtown, in an area filled with vagrants, drug addicts, prostitutes, and lots of violence. I used to head to the church office around 4:00 a.m. every Sunday to pray and prepare before the services began. The front door to the church as well as the door to my office opened right onto the street.

One Sunday morning during my first winter in Phoenix, I was in my office before the break of dawn when suddenly I was startled by a violent *bang* on the door. Being new to the area and scared to death, I decided not to answer the pounding. But it continued on and on. Even though the blinds were drawn, the person out there probably saw the light on inside my office. I couldn't get anything done with all that racket, so I resolved to just open the door a crack and see what was going on. But as soon as I cracked the door to take a peek, the guy on the other side pushed it open and forced his way inside. He had long, greasy hair, his face was smeared with dirt, he smelled like liquor and human waste, and his clothes were ragged and filthy. He stood uncomfortably close to me and bellowed, "I want money! I want money!"

Welcome to the big city! At first I thought he was robbing me. He kept yelling at me, half crazed, "I want money!" Once he added that he needed something to eat. I wasn't buying that line, so I tried to confidently back him down. "I'm not going to give you money for your drugs or alcohol. I won't do that."

But he was relentless—and I was stuck. On the spur of the moment, I decided to make a deal—and possibly begin a road to recovery with him. "I'll tell you what I'll do. If you will stay here and go to church with me, after church I'll take you out and buy you a meal like you've never had."

His eyes narrowed as he considered the offer. His reply was surprisingly logical—and not dismissive. "Look at me!" he yelled with a trace of anger. "Nobody wants to sit by me. I'm dirty and I smell bad. Look at me."

I paused for a second, then upped the ante. "Well, how about this? I'll let you take a shower in the bathroom by my office. While you shower I'll go home and get you one of my suits and bring it back for you to wear."

He agreed to the deal. I got him situated, then ran out to my car to drive home. It was about twenty minutes away, which gave me time to think more clearly. As I sped west, I chastised myself for my plan. *He won't even be there when I get back. And he might steal everything that's not nailed down. What a fool I am to do this. My office will smell awful, and he'll probably leave the door wide open, giving every other homeless person in the area an open invitation to loot the place. This is crazy.*

By the time I returned with a suit and other articles of clothing, I was so angry at myself for being so naive. But when I entered my office, there he was, standing in the middle of the room with a towel wrapped around him. After I recovered from the shock, I handed over the clothing. He dressed in the bathroom and emerged without the tie, which he didn't know how to tie. I tied it for him, put some greasy kid's stuff on his hair, and had him looking like a Philadelphia lawyer.

Everything else went smoothly during the service, and he sat there in the audience, quite attentive. That morning I preached to one person: him. When I gave the altar call, he came to the altar weeping. Afterward I took him out and bought him a nice meal.

After he left, he returned to his family's house. He told his family, including his brother, Jack, who was a very sharp young man. Jack was moved by what had happened, and he came to our church and got saved too! Jack was so transformed by his experience with God that he went off to Bible school, then returned to Phoenix and became an associate pastor at our church.

Later he moved to Detroit, where he grew a large church, attracting thousands of people every week, and that congregation loved him. Jack invited me to preach for him many times, which I did. His church donated thousands of dollars to the Dream Center and felt very connected to that work. Sadly, Jack died unexpectedly on a speaking trip he took to the Netherlands, but he left a great legacy.

It all started with that half hour of terror and confusion I spent with his brother—the risk I took. The sad addendum to the story is that Jack's brother went back to his old ways, back to the streets. But his story is not finished yet.

Use your half hours to risk wisely, and you'll make a real difference in your world.

30

ACT!

Half-Hour Power Principle:
Follow God into His amazing adventure for you.

E very great person of God whom we read about in the Bible, from Abraham to Esther to Paul, was a person of action. One of the traits that enabled their choices to generate substantial and lasting results was their willingness to think outside the box and do the unexpected. Whether their actions had to do with battlefield strategies, facing down a king, or preaching examples, the great ones never took the expected or easy route.

When Jesus calls us to bear fruit in this life, He is prompting us to demonstrate our faith by relying on Him and taking courses of action that defy the wisdom of the world. As former president Jimmy Carter exhorts us, "Go out on a limb. That's where the fruit is."[20]

You will be amazed at how God can use just thirty minutes of your time to lead you on a journey that may push you out of your comfort zone but ultimately will bear tremendous fruit.

FOLLOW GOD'S LEAD

When I pastored in Iowa, the church we grew there was based on the same principles and strategies that had enabled my dad to develop his church into one of the largest in the Assemblies of God denomination. He did a lot of outreach activities and creative programming. Most important, he simply loved on people. That's what I had seen and been part of all my life, so when we built our church in Davenport, Iowa, we used those same approaches. It was greatly blessed by the Lord.

But when I had the sense that I was supposed to move to Phoenix, I also had an itch to build the new church differently. Rather than do things the way my earthly father had, I was determined to try to build a new church the way my heavenly Father wanted me to do it. But what did that mean?

So I prayed, "Lord Jesus, I want to build this church the way You would build it. How would You build it?" I began to study the scriptures to figure out what gets His attention, and, of course, passage after passage demonstrated the answer.

- A crying baby got His attention.
- A dying sparrow got His attention.
- A hungry vulture got His attention.
- The coin that the poor widow put into the offering box got His attention.
- The woman dying of a hemorrhage got His attention.
- The thief on the cross got His attention.

It didn't take much discernment on my part to see that the most vulnerable and undesirable people grabbed His attention—those whom He created but who were the castoffs of society captivated His heart. That's how we decided that our focus would be on ministering to the people that nobody wanted; if we could bring them to church, then we would capture God's attention.

When at first I described that strategy to people in our church, some laughed at me. So we put people in wheelchairs in the front row and did other unusual things like that. Many observers thought it was a travesty.

One day during the time we were implementing this approach at our church, a soft-spoken man came to my office to see me. His name was Walt Rattray. After the introductions, he got right to the point: "Pastor, I've been kicked out of the last three churches I've gone to. The reason is I bring men who live on the street to church with me and the churches don't want them."

We talked for a while, then I told him, "I like what you do, Walt. I want those people here. In fact, I have some buses out here that are not being used. If you want them, you could use them to bring your men." We talked it through a bit more and agreed to go for it.

True to his word, Walt brought in three busloads of guys from the street that first week. I was unaware of their arrival until I suddenly heard an awful commotion in the auditorium. I went running down the hall to see what had happened. As I entered the sanctuary, I ran right into Walt. The first words out of his mouth were, "Pastor, you don't want me to come back here anymore, do you?" I still didn't know what was going on, but it was a few minutes before the service was due to start, so I needed to get to the bottom of things quickly: I asked him what had happened.

> People attract people. It doesn't
> matter what kind of people they are.

Walt got a real pained look on his face and said, "Well, a drunk guy that we brought got up in the pulpit and started preaching. He was under the spirit all right." I couldn't help but smile. In fact, my biggest concern was whether the guy had preached a better sermon than I was planning for that Sunday! I put my arm on Walt's shoulder, looked him in the eye, and said, "Walt, listen to me. This is the risk we knew we were taking when we decided to pursue the people that nobody else wants. So, yes, I do want you and your men to come back. And, Walt, next week I'll give you six buses."

Some people would say that was the dumbest thing they'd ever heard. But what I had discovered is that people attract people. It doesn't matter what kind of people they are. So we increased our efforts to reach the people that nobody wanted. That caused us to lose a lot of the people who had been part of the congregation—and it didn't faze us in the least. We were trying to follow the lead of Jesus, who hung out with the lower class of people and was rejected by the elites.

After some time, the word got out about this crazy church that was taking in the undesirables, and suddenly we began to attract the people that all the churches wanted. We found ourselves appealing to a few of the millionaires in the city, wealthy people who had a heart for the community and were willing to invest in a vision to address the tough problems in the city at a grassroots level. We began to exhort our church members to "find a need and fill it."

Walt really changed my life in that thirty-minute meeting in my office when he offered to bring the undesirables to our church. That put the heart into our ministry.

THE BIRTH OF THE DREAM CENTER

Later, Walt started a place called The Church on the Street, which was the original Dream Center but without a good facility. Eventually we changed the name of the ministry to the Dream Center and bought the old Embassy Suites hotel in Phoenix as the facility—a church with a swimming pool, elevators, and the whole works. Today we have hundreds of street people being saved, going through rehab programs, and getting job training and housing assistance. It all started with that thirty-minute meeting and Walt's simple offer.

And our church has continued to grow prolifically over the years, because we try to find needs and fill them. When I find a need, I jump up and click my heels and yell, "Praise God!" because it's another chance to demonstrate the love of God by helping hurting people.

It's an opportunity to act.

IT'S UP TO YOU

If you accept the fact that God created us to be agents of transformation and realize that every day He gives us opportunities to change the world in little but meaningful ways, then the half hours that you have to work with can produce great outcomes. Bringing about positive transformation is never easy and rarely quick. But it is always satisfying. *You just have to act.*

To fulfill God's purpose in your life, you have to take action; sometimes that action will involve risk. If you're a leader, many, if not most, of your decisions will involve significant risks. If you're a parent, many of the things you do for your children and family will involve risk. If you're passionate about a cause that you're involved in, progress will involve risk. Without taking those risks, you won't get too far. Knowing what risks to take is between you and God; He'll provide the guidance if you'll provide the ear and the effort.

I have to confess that I get tired of hearing people say that they're not doing anything about a situation because they're "waiting on the Lord." Too often that becomes an excuse to do nothing. Yes, it's important to move in God's timing and rhythm, but while you're waiting, you also need to be preparing for action, whatever that action might turn out to be.

I think about the sprinter who is lined up at the starting blocks, feet in place, fingers on the ground, eyes looking down the track—he's waiting for the starting gun to go off, but he's ready for action the moment the shot is fired. You need to be like that too: ready for action at the appropriate moment, using your time to be prepared to maximize the opportunity.

So are you getting results by being ready and taking action when the time is right? Are you taking intelligent risks that enhance your results? Here's something for you to try that might be helpful in your self-evaluation. At the end of every day, ask yourself what risks you took that day. If you can identify one or more courses of action that required meaningful risk, then you are making progress. If you cannot identify any, then you probably have little to show for the day and must question whether you are still open to personal growth and whether you are really trusting God.

Everyone I know who has been successful in life has been willing to take action and intelligent risks. To experience real joy, excitement, growth, and wisdom, you have to get your hands dirty in the nitty-gritty of producing results—and trying some things that could really put you over the top along the way.

It all can begin with just thirty minutes…

The power of a half hour!

Half-Hour Power Principles

1. Thirty minutes can wreck or redeem a life.
2. Small time investments produce huge returns.
3. Knowing why you are "here" brings deep satisfaction.
4. Align your values with God's values.
5. Use the tools from your God-given kit.
6. Pursue the best relationship imaginable.
7. Be honest and transparent with your best Friend.
8. When visiting with God, don't do all the talking.
9. Go "low" so God can lift you "high."
10. Forgiveness brings freedom.
11. Shift your outlook to change your destiny.
12. Make being thankful a habit.
13. Step off your treadmill to get perspective.
14. Obeying God leads to satisfaction.
15. Your dreams are God's dreams for you.
16. Preparation includes ample perspiration.
17. Boost productivity with thirty-minute meetings.
18. Be creative...like your heavenly Dad.
19. Hope results from God's grace and your effort.
20. You exist for other people.
21. Good friendships require time...over time.
22. Thirty-minute encounters benefit every marriage.
23. Children need a large quantity of quality time.
24. Build character in children by showing them yours.
25. Life is hard—we must help each other.
26. Help make your church relevant.
27. Take opportunities to share God's love.
28. Practice giving until you get really good at it.
29. Take a risk for God—what could be safer?
30. Follow God into His amazing adventure for you.

Personal Power of a Half Hour
Action Plan

Personal Action Plan #1

Reading Assignment—Chapter 1: Change Your Destiny

(*) **Half-Hour Power Principle:** *Thirty minutes can wreck or redeem a life.*
Both wonderful and terrible things can occur during thirty-minute blocks of time. We can use them to study the Bible, encourage friends, or play with a child. Or we can use them for sinful purposes. There is great power in only thirty minutes!

Inspiration from Tommy
"Armed with the Word of God and the ears to hear what God would like to say to you through His Holy Spirit, things can change radically for the better if you're willing to invest that little amount of time into getting things right with God."

(*) **The Plan/Action Steps**
1. Write down thoughts or ideas that came to mind as you read about Carl and what happened to him during thirty minutes.
2. How have your activities during thirty-minute periods of time influenced your life? the lives of other people you know well?
3. Which steps will you take to spend more time hearing what God might desire to say to you about your use of short blocks of time? Which step(s) will you start taking *today*?

Personal Action Plan #2

Reading Assignment—Chapter 2: Why Time Matters

◯ **Half-Hour Power Principle:** *Small time investments produce huge returns.* Our lives are a gift from God, who gives us the precious and nonrenewable gift of time. Using our time carefully, intentionally, wisely, and productively to organize our lives honors His plan for each of us and blesses Him with the results.

With each passing minute, our time on earth is winding down. No wonder God provided us with verses focusing on being faithful with time—including little half hours.

Inspiration from Tommy

"Time is the most significant nonrenewable resource at our disposal.... When God gave this gift, He intended for us to use it carefully, intentionally, wisely, and productively."

◯ **The Plan/Action Steps**

1. What came to mind concerning your own view of time and how you use or abuse it? Why?

2. In what ways do people try to avoid thinking about how brief life on Earth really is, and how has their influence affected your view and use of time?

3. Write down a thirty-minute block of time that impacted your life— positively or negatively—and then commit to using thirty minutes within the next twenty-four hours (1) to connect in a special way with God; (2) do something special for a friend or loved one; or (3) enjoy an activity that makes you smile.

Personal Action Plan #3

Reading Assignment—Chapter 3: Clarify Your Vision and Purpose

◔ **Half-Hour Power Principle:** *Knowing why you are "here" brings deep satisfaction.*

When we each discover God's unique vision for us—why we are here—it inspires, energizes, challenges, and consumes us. It also makes life much more interesting and fun!

God often reveals His vision during focused half hours, when we humbly seek it and are committed to faithfully carrying out His assignments.

Often He reveals His direction for us when we are young. And He connects our lives with other people who will be part of His grand plan for advancing His kingdom. Zealously pursuing His vision with conviction and confidence establishes our respective purpose and goals in life.

Inspiration from Tommy

"There is no higher calling you can have than to receive and tirelessly pursue God's unique vision for you."

◔ **The Plan/Action Steps**

1. Write down God's vision for why you are here. If you don't yet know it—and the sense of purpose it provides—how deeply do you desire it? Why?

2. Set aside a half hour to:
   - Humbly talk with God about your willingness to fulfill His unique vision for you.
   - Write down indications God has given you, perhaps at a young age, of His vision—and assignment—for you.

3. During future half hours, pray about God's vision for you and fulfilling the assignment represented by that vision.

Personal Action Plan #4

Reading Assignment—Chapter 4: Solidify Your Values

◎ **Half-Hour Power Principle:** *Align your values with God's values.*

It's easy for us to define our values by external influences such as peers, family members, the media, and even personal experiences. Also, internal pressures caused by bad thinking or out-of-control feelings may also define the values by which we live. So it's important for us to reflect on values we actually live out daily rather than those we "are supposed" to live out.

God knows that we'll experience much better lives and have greater impact for His kingdom if we pursue and apply His values.

Inspiration from Tommy

"What really matters in life is what's important to God. His values need to be our values."

◎ **The Plan/Action Steps**

1. What would a video of your behavior during the past two weeks, combined with an analysis of your checking account during the past two months, reveal about your values? Where do most or all of your values come from?

2. Set aside a half hour:
   - Reflect on everything you'd like to do before you die. Then compare this list to God's values found in the Bible.
   - Write down what you discover during this process about your key values and God's key values.
   - Think about and then write down the consequences created when God's values have not been your values. *(Note: If you need more time, set aside another half hour to complete this.)*

Personal Action Plan #5

Reading Assignment—Chapter 5: Sharpen Your Gifts and Abilities

◔ **Half-Hour Power Principle:** *Use the tools from your God-given kit.*
Opportunities for serving God are *virtually* unlimited—being a loving spouse or parent, teaching children, praying for friends, helping less-fortunate people,…

Having called you to His service, God gave you talents—various gifts and abilities—to use in blessing other people for His glory as you fulfill your God-given purpose. This mix of spiritual gifts, combined with "supercharged" gifts from the Holy Spirit if you love Jesus as Lord and Savior, becomes even more strategic and influential when you invest in developing and sharpening them using half-hour power. Many biblical characters, no different from us, took their God-given gifts seriously and refined them greatly.

Inspiration from Tommy
"What happens when you commit yourself to maturing your gifts? You become capable of accomplishing superior outcomes…. better equipped, more efficient, and undeniably successful thanks to your commitment to growing your gifts."

◔ **The Plan/Action Steps**
1. In a half hour:
   - Ask God for wisdom, then list your God-given talents—gifts and abilities. (You might consult godly people who know you well, using other half hours.)
   - Devote a half hour every day—or even once a week—to honing your gifts and abilities by interviewing people, playing music, reading, doing Internet research, and so on.
   - Prayerfully ask for and seek ways to better use your talents—gifts and abilities—for God's service.

Personal Action Plan #6

Reading Assignment—Chapter 6: Make a Regular Connection

◐ **Half-Hour Power Principle:** *Pursue the best relationship imaginable.*
God desires your passionate love and will draw near to you when you draw near to Him. When you consistently invest half hours in being alone with God—humbly talking with Him, thanking and praising Him, reading His eternal Word—not only does your thinking get headed in the right direction, you also build an intimate, dynamic, two-way relationship with Him.

Your half hours with God may be different from that of another Jesus follower. What's important is developing personal spiritual habits that keep God in first place in your life.

Inspiration from Tommy
"Thirty minutes alone with God will change your life.... And the more consistently you spend time and thought addressing His words to you, the deeper understanding you'll achieve and the greater your love for Him and His Word will be."

◐ The Plan/Action Steps
1. In a half hour:
   - Honestly ponder your relationship with God: your commitment, attitudes and actions that hinder deeper intimacy with Him.
   - Ask God to guide you in developing or enhancing your intimacy with Him.
   - Explore the balance of prayer, Bible exploration, and thanking and praising Him, whether or not this is a new spiritual habit.
   - Devote at least a half hour daily to your relationship with God.

Personal Action Plan #7

Reading Assignment—Chapter 7: Friends "Hang Out"

(♪) **Half-Hour Power Principle:** *Be honest and transparent with your best Friend.*

How do you approach God—the King of kings, the Creator of the universe—when entering His presence through prayer? How open are you in His presence?

If you follow Jesus, God has given you the Holy Spirit, who aids you in praying. Prayer is to be a significant and holy event during your half hours with God.

Regularly praying during half hours will transform your relationship with God, including your understanding of and experience with the Holy Spirit. Tommy wrote, "My time praying…is a time when I receive a sense of peace in my heart from spending time with God and sensing Him at work in my life."

Inspiration from Tommy

"I treat prayer as if I am spending time with my best friend.… The Holy Spirit has become a friend and a prayer partner—one who has completely altered my life.… [God] is such a creative and available listener and friend!"

(♪) **The Plan/Action Steps**
1. During your private, daily half hours with God:
   - Prepare yourself to enter God's holy presence.
   - Praise God and invite the Holy Spirit to be your prayer partner.
   - Be honest and transparent with God, allowing Him to touch your heart and mind in intimate ways.

Personal Action Plan #8

Reading Assignment—Chapter 8: Listen

① **Half-Hour Power Principle:** *When visiting with God, don't do all the talking.*

God still speaks to His people today. When you are silent, still, and receptive to Him during half hours, He will communicate with you. And He will actually tailor His messages to who you are and your situation, and in ways you can understand, to give you insights and wisdom you need to successfully fulfill the tasks He has given you.

He may use an audible voice, visions, Bible passages, or words from other believers. Yet it's easy to skip this time of stillness and rationalize the need to be busy and "productive" instead.

Inspiration from Tommy

"No matter how [God] chooses to speak to you, you can be quite certain that you won't hear Him at all if you're always talking and busy."

① **The Plan/Action Steps**

1. During your next private, quiet, daily half hour with God:
   - Write down what you really believe about God—His ability and desire to guide you effectively and how He has revealed His guidance in the past to you or to someone else.
   - Ask God to help you be still before Him during half hours—and other times—and to believe His promises.
   - Practice readiness to receive God's "marching orders"—wherever they come from!
   - Write down what God reveals—and then do it.

Personal Action Plan #9

Reading Assignment—Chapter 9: Humble Yourself

○ **Half-Hour Power Principle:** *Go "low" so God can lift you "high."*
God highly values an attitude of humility, and so did many biblical characters. Each of us can use half hours to become more humble, to rid ourselves of a pride-filled sense of self-worth.

  With God's help, we can honestly assess ourselves—our strengths and weaknesses—and learn to develop a sincere spirit of humility coming from our hearts that God can use to bless us and everyone we meet!

Inspiration from Tommy
"There are two types of people in this world: those who come into a room and say, 'Well, here I am!' and those who come in and say, 'Aha, there you are.' Which type are you?"

○ **The Plan/Action Steps**
  1. Ask God to give you the sincere desire to pursue humility.
  2. Consider ways you can practice humility in a half hour or less:
     • Say phrases or respond in ways that indicate you are nothing special or that your action deserves no special recognition.
     • Sincerely compliment and give credit to people who work with you on projects.
     • Listen to what's on other people's minds, and encourage them.
     • Apologize readily for your mistakes and wrong actions.
     • Thank people who have helped you grow, adding value to your life.
     • When appropriate, embrace other people's ideas and think of them more highly than your own.

Personal Action Plan #10

Reading Assignment—Chapter 10: Repent and Forgive

Ⓛ **Half-Hour Power Principle:** *Forgiveness brings freedom.*
Every day we face important choices. Whether or not to quickly and willingly forgive people who seek our forgiveness. Whether or not to quickly and willingly repent—turn away from—errors we commit. Whether or not to hold grudges or use other people in selfish, manipulative ways.

It's vital that we use half hours to allow God to speak to us about such matters and then respond in biblical ways. After all, God takes issues of forgiveness seriously (see Matthew 6:14–15).

Inspiration from Tommy
"Regularly take a half hour and ask the Lord to bring to your awareness any people whom you need to forgive."

Ⓛ **The Plan/Action Steps**
After reviewing the letter sent to Tommy, take the following steps:
1. Ask for forgiveness.
   • In a half hour, list names of any person(s) you remember having wronged—but never asked for forgiveness.
   • What do you notice in reviewing your list? Which thought pattern(s) and actions often surface?
   • What hindered you from asking these people for forgiveness?
   • Contact these people and ask for forgiveness.
2. List any person(s) you need to forgive, and prayerfully forgive each one. Start doing this whether or not these people have actually come to you and asked for your forgiveness.

Personal Action Plan #11

Reading Assignment—Chapter 11: Own a Great Attitude

(◡) **Half-Hour Power Principle:** *Shift your outlook to change your destiny.*
Attitude plays a key role in changing our destiny, and even a half hour can be long enough to readjust negative attitudes, especially if we each own—accept responsibility for—our attitude. Think about Jesus's creativity, love, confidence, compassion… He came to Earth to demonstrate godliness, and we can imitate His attitude.

Chuck Swindoll explained the importance of attitude this way: "I am convinced that life is 10 percent what happens to me and 90 percent how I react to it. And so it is with you. We are in charge of our attitudes."

Inspiration from Tommy
"Every hour of every day you are making choices about the attitude you adopt.… And the great thing is that an attitude can be changed. But sometimes we need to stop for a half hour and do an attitude adjustment."

(◡) **The Plan/Action Steps**
1. Set aside a half hour, then complete these steps:
   - Reflect on and write down words people closest to you would use to describe your attitude.
   - Consider how you will benefit from using thirty-minute opportunities that arise throughout your life to improve attitude, then write them down.
   - Think about a mentor, friend, or family member who might help you improve any attitude that hinders—self-doubt, fear, complacency— then write a letter asking for that person's assistance.

Personal Action Plan #12

Reading Assignment—Chapter 12: Practice "Gr–attitude"

(◌) **Half-Hour Power Principle:** *Make being thankful a habit.*
Our subconscious habits—thinking, behavior, belief—produce our attitudes.
Yet it's so easy for us to not be intentionally grateful for God's love and faithfulness, exciting opportunities, the people in our lives, our possessions, our skills and abilities.

Investing thirty minutes to express gratitude will change your outlook on life—for today and in the future.

Ways you express gratitude may include writing letters of appreciation to your parents, thanking your coworkers for their good work, and bringing joy into a room with uplifting words. And, of course, thanking God for His blessings—His presence, insights, protection, forgiveness, as well as your loved ones, your job, your talents.

Inspiration from Tommy
"Don't forget to thank God too!… The thirty minutes we invest in acknowledging God's presence and engagement in our lives and activities is a crucial factor in creating a permanent bond with Him."

(◌) **The Plan/Action Steps**
1. List some people who have said encouraging words to you or done encouraging things for you. (Listening to you during challenging times, helping you complete a difficult task, providing excellent service, encouraging your child, and so on.)
2. Discover ways to demonstrate gratitude to these people in practical ways—and then put your thankfulness into practice.
3. Ask God to help you make a habit of being thankful with people in every area of your life.

Personal Action Plan #13

Reading Assignment—Chapter 13: Slow Down

◔ **Half-Hour Power Principle:** *Step off your treadmill to get perspective.*
Many of us stay busy to avoid dealing with life's tough situations. Consider how obsessed people are with entertainment, for example, and how preoccupied they try to be with their electronic gadgets.

Yes, setting aside half hours with God in order to be quiet and make sense of turbulence and challenge is difficult, especially in light of noises and distractions. We can learn much from Jesus, who modeled the ability to remain calm during chaos.

We must learn to value times of reflection, stillness, and self-debriefing—or we won't choose to get off the treadmill and get perspective.

Inspiration from Tommy
"One of the benefits of being still before God is the opportunity to reflect on how fortunate we are today—and to know what we are called to do and to be every day."

◔ **The Plan/Action Steps**
1. Whether or not you have been setting aside time for stillness and quiet, take the time today to reflect on the answers to these questions:
   - How can you spend more time being still and quiet, enhancing your ability to hear from God and to focus on Him?
   - What unnecessary noises and activities disrupt and hinder your pursuit of God and His greatest dream for your life, and how can you reduce their harmful impact?
   - Will you ask God to help you to slow down in the future?
   - What person in your life might be willing to assist you in valuing and creating half hours of tranquility to focus on what really matters?

Personal Action Plan #14

Reading Assignment—Chapter 14: When God Calls...Answer "Yes"

(!) **Half-Hour Power Principle:** *Obeying God leads to satisfaction.*

When God asks you to do something, obey and say yes. This may seem simple, yet its implications are profound. Sometimes what He asks us to do is simple, such as e-mailing someone or helping a neighbor. Sometimes He asks us to do difficult things—and even suffer for His glory. His requests may seem to make no sense, which might cause us to resist His call. So we need to trust what the Holy Spirit whispers in our hearts.

God loves us dearly and unfolds His plans for us for our good!

Inspiration from Tommy

"Getting on board as quickly as possible when [God] asks us to do something is such a smart—make that *wise*—response. It's not always easy, but we need to... just do it."

(!) **The Plan/Action Steps**

1. In a half hour:
   - Think about how God has communicated to you: in His Word, through followers of Jesus, inner promptings by the Holy Spirit, and so on.
   - Ponder your willingness to obey God no matter what the consequences may be, and what may be holding you back from completely trusting Him.
   - Ask God to make you more sensitive to His leading and more willing to obey Him, no matter how many excuses may come to mind.

Personal Action Plan #15

Reading Assignment—Chapter 15: Follow Your Passion

(!) **Half-Hour Power Principle:** *Your dreams are God's dreams for you.*
How might your half hours foster your passion and dreams? And how much risk and how many action steps might you be required to take in faith?

Fortunately you do not have to know all the answers to these and other questions far in advance. What's important is realizing that your dreams—hopes, expectations, desires, goals, objectives—are God's dreams for you! He longs to open up incredible opportunities for you.

Inspiration from Tommy
"God loves to fulfill the dreams in us He birthed."

(!) **The Plan/Action Steps**
1. Ponder how much vision you think God has concerning your dreams.
   - What is your understanding of God and His desires for you?
   - To what extent do you *really* believe that God loves to fulfill the dreams in you that He has birthed?
2. Without editing your ideas, write down things you'd like to do *with God.* These may be small or huge, even seemingly impossible.
3. Pray, asking for God's wisdom, strength, power…to encourage your passion to do great things with Him.

Personal Action Plan #16

Reading Assignment—Chapter 16: Prepare for Success

(!) **Half-Hour Power Principle:** *Preparation includes ample perspiration.*
Sufficient preparation plays a key role in accomplishing great things. More often than not, people who figure out what it takes to come out on top and do what is necessary to make that happen become winners in life. They commit themselves to readiness.

We each have different tasks to perform in order to fulfill our unique calling from God. Successful authors, for example, do the hard work of preparing to write potential bestsellers. Pastors prepare for the chance to share truths from God's Word effectively.

By preparing your heart, mind, and body, you can improve your chances for success. And if this becomes a habit, your life will be more productive, enjoyable, and meaningful.

Inspiration from Tommy
"We all have different tasks to perform in order to fulfill our unique calling from God."

(!) **The Plan/Action Steps**
1. Reflect on one still-in-your-mind meaningful task you'd like to achieve but have never taken practical steps toward achieving.
   - Use half hours to sharpen your perspectives and start preparing— studying, reflecting, building relationships, honing a particular skill, inviting God to be part of your efforts, thanking Him for enabling you… As you work toward your goal, focus on spiritual, mental, and physical preparation.
   - Commit yourself to continual preparation for success in accomplishing each task you undertake.

Personal Action Plan #17

Reading Assignment—Chapter 17: Make a Career "Work"

ⓘ **Half-Hour Power Principle:** *Boost productivity with thirty-minute meetings.* Often when a particular problem at work stymies us, someone else has an effective solution! And a half-hour meeting—during lunch or another time—gives us opportunities to develop effective solutions through creative problem solving with people of like heart. We don't fritter away hours spent in worry and unproductive problem grappling.

In order for half hours to work and to use participants' time efficiently, the leader(s) needs to be adequately prepared and practice discussion management during each half hour. Sometimes longer meetings are necessary, but you can make them exceptions, not the norm. Short meetings enable people to prepare for their responsibilities and support everyone else's efforts, encourage and mentor people, and set people up for success.

Certainly it's important to keep God in the loop, asking Him for wisdom and guidance!

Inspiration from Tommy
"Some good, old-fashioned conversation with friends and colleagues can put you back on a productive track within thirty minutes."

ⓘ **The Plan/Action Steps**
1. In half hours:
   - Evaluate your problem-solving habits, particularly noting how much time you spend on difficult problems and how often you seek wise counsel from others.
   - Set aside half hours to intentionally address specific, difficult problems—on your own and with others.
   - Refine your half-hour approach in order to keep accomplishing more and building even stronger relationships with people and God.

Personal Action Plan #18

Reading Assignment—Chapter 18: Activate Your Creativity

◔ **Half-Hour Power Principle:** *Be creative...like your heavenly Dad.*
By focusing your attention during even one half hour, you can tap into your God-given creativity. Perhaps, like the man Tommy described, you write one page a day for a book. Or express your worship through painting as a gift to God. You might sing to God, expressing your gratitude to Him for all He has done in, through, and for you and the people you love.

Some particularly artistic people use focused, creative half hours to empty themselves of deep but otherwise inexpressible feelings for their heavenly Father. Imagine how precious those expressions are to God, the One who has given us our creativity!

Inspiration from Tommy
"When you have something to express to God, use some creative gift He has given you" during half hours.

◔ **The Plan/Action Steps**
1. Reflect on your creativity, then ask God to help you set aside half hours to express it. (Even if you think you are not creative, God will likely guide you in discovering or rediscovering creativity.)
2. Begin to plan half-hour creative sessions when you focus attention on creativity and do not judge how well you express it. This is a time for you and God, not a time of comparison to other people's creativity.
3. If you feel comfortable doing so, invite a friend to be creative with you! Who knows where that may lead!

Personal Action Plan #19

Reading Assignment—Chapter 19: Sustain Hope

◯ **Half-Hour Power Principle:** *Hope results from God's grace and your effort.*
Without hope, dreams wither. Unfortunately, many people today base their
hope on persons, places, things…rather than on God. And during overwhelming
circumstances, they lose sight of the big picture of life.

God's gift of hope is essential, and sometimes nurturing this hope—getting
it into our heads and hearts—requires work.

Which strategies energize our hope and provide perspectives empowering us
to overcome every obstacle? Reading the Bible daily. Pondering what Jesus has
done for us and God's plans for us. Praying that the Holy Spirit will completely
control our lives, then releasing control to God.

Half hours with the God of creation encourage hope, as does accepting
encouragement from other people who support our efforts to obey God. Encouraging
other people also cultivates hope.

Inspiration from Tommy
"If you tie your hope to the power and love of God, then you can endure the
difficulties of life, become a person of character who recognizes his own insufficiency
without Christ—and have an unshakable hope when Jesus is at the center
of your existence."

◯ **The Plan/Action Steps**
1. Read the Bible daily, receiving God's instruction, reinforcing words,
   and encouragement.
2. Ask the Holy Spirit to control your life and give you hope.
3. Continually accept encouragement from other people, and find
   people to encourage. During half hours, ask God to enable you to
   help somebody else.

Personal Action Plan #20

Reading Assignment—Chapter 20: Bless Others

◯ **Half-Hour Power Principle:** *You exist for other people.*

Jesus, a man of action, calls us to fully love God and people. And He described love that takes action and improves people's lives. His belief in lovingly serving people motivated Him to surrender everything for our sake.

You have the immeasurable opportunity to build up other people using words, gifts, a listening ear, willingness to commit time… You have the responsibility to live as a servant, seeking ways of blessing God and others.

You can, in God's power and demonstrating Jesus's love, inspire people to live more meaningfully and productively, supporting their efforts in doing what God calls them to do. God blesses us so we can bless others! With His help, blessing others can become a wonderful habit.

Inspiration from Tommy

"The beauty of building up people is that you can have a lifelong positive impact on somebody in just thirty minutes. I know because people have done it for me, and I've done it for them."

◯ **The Plan/Action Steps**

1. Think about when you have given love away. What happened to the other person? to you and your capacity to love? Why?

2. Which people, if you gave each a focused half hour of time, could you love and encourage? Ask God to guide and empower you in giving love away all the time!

3. Why is sincere, godly love so powerful?

Personal Action Plan #21

Reading Assignment—Chapter 21: Connect with Impact

◑ **Half-Hour Power Principle:** *Good friendships require time...over time.*
Our relationships are precious, and deep ones usually take time to build. Each of us invests considerable commitment, energy, and time in building genuine friendships.

So building relationships is certainly one of the best ways to use the power of a half hour. When we consistently invest thirty minutes in people, even with those who do not reciprocate, we are demonstrating the love of Jesus and applying God's biblical truths. Many people around us struggle with serious issues and need to experience God's peace and purpose. We are, in effect, Jesus's hands and feet!

Inspiration from Tommy
"The more intentional you are about using your half hours wisely, the more likely you will be to develop a solid community of relationships founded on your willingness to devote time to those people."

◑ **The Plan/Action Steps**
1. Reflect on your deeper, genuine relationships and ways in which you cultivated them. What do you notice? How often have people used the power of a half hour with you?
2. List people in your circle of influence who you would like to know better, who are in need and perhaps open to relationship with you, and who have expressed interest in getting to know you better. Then begin using half hours to connect with some of these people.

Personal Action Plan #22

Reading Assignment—Chapter 22: Strengthen Marriage

(♪) **Half-Hour Power Principle:** *Thirty-minute encounters benefit every marriage.*

It's no secret that marriage, though ordained by God, has many stresses and strains. Spouses have different backgrounds, views of money and child rearing, ways of handling conflict. Yet, if you are married or planning to marry, the power of half hours can do much to improve the health and well-being of your marriage. Such thirty-minute blocks of time provide opportunities for conflict resolution, basic communication, and other benefits. As Tommy shared, a half hour can be a game changer.

In this increasingly stress-filled culture, it's important for couples to set aside time to just *be* with each other. To listen, discuss, plan, share hopes and dreams… with cell phones turned off.

Inspiration from Tommy

"Marriage is a challenge for anyone, but even small investments in communication and in conflict resolution can vastly improve the health of your covenant relationship."

(♪) **The Plan/Action Steps**

1. Whether you are married or engaged, list steps you can take right now to capture half hours during which you and your loved one can relax and invest in your relationship. Pray together, asking God for wisdom and guidance in this area.

   • Place half hours on your calendars or cell phones—and start investing in your relationship, thirty minutes at a time!

   • If you already set aside time regularly to be with your spouse or future spouse, discover ways to make these times even more fun and productive.

Personal Action Plan #23

Reading Assignment—Chapter 23: Build a Healthy Family

(♪) **Half-Hour Power Principle:** *Children need a large quantity of quality time.* Strangely, family relationships cause lots of stress. You can reduce stress and strengthen your family by consistently investing half hours in family members.

It's vital to guard family time and devote yourself to family members collectively and individually during prescribed family hours. Tips on building up your family include: listen to what is said, directly or indirectly; be fully present with loved ones; establish thirty-minute routines, such as eating dinner together, doing fun activities, or discussing world events.

Inspiration from Tommy

"Your family—your spouse and your children—require both the best time you can give them and as much time as you can give them.... Look for those extra half hours that you can devote to them that represent quality time while increasing the quantity of time shared with them."

(♪) **The Plan/Action Steps**

1. Set aside a half hour to reflect on how and when your family interacts regularly together.
   - What changes might you make to your family time? (Hint: what does your calendar reveal about your priorities? about quantity and quality time spent with family?)
   - If you have children at home or living near you, how might you use half hours to focus attention on them—collectively and individually?
   - What specific steps will you take to do this—starting today?

Personal Action Plan #24

Reading Assignment—Chapter 24: Raise Kids Right

(!) **Half-Hour Power Principle:** *Build character in children by showing them yours.*

How much difference will thirty minutes make in a child's life? A lot. Throwing a ball, discussing a problem at school, providing homework guidance—powerful half-hour opportunities are endless.

Half hours are about deepening and strengthening your relationships—what really matters. Think of the opportunities to help children develop godly character and spiritual understanding of God's principles from life experiences. Tell stories that illustrate the importance of accepting responsibility for one's behavior. Discuss your child's media use and the content of media choices. When your child's attention wanes, move on.

Inspiration from Tommy

"If your kids give you thirty minutes, take it!... And because families are the cornerstone of the church, what better investment could you make than devoting yourself to the needs of your family?"

(!) **The Plan/Action Steps**

1. Make a conscious effort to naturally and strategically use half hours to connect with your child and create teaching opportunities.

   • Use your child's interests and struggles, as well as your life experiences and stories, to teach godly character traits.

   • Watch for teaching moments on the important issues in life, then create simple statements summarizing the spirit of each lesson.

   • Teach God's principles in daily conversations about everyday events.

Personal Action Plan #25

Reading Assignment—Chapter 25: People Are Just People

(♩) **Half-Hour Power Principle:** *Life is hard—we must help each other.*
None of us is perfect. We all fail and get discouraged. And it's important to accept other people for who they are. A struggling person, for example, is God's gift to us—someone into whom we can pour our lives. And it's vital to keep our eyes on Jesus, who never fails, so we don't fail people we could have blessed. When we experience difficulty, how wonderful it is when someone affirms that we are loved and lovable and helps us.

We each appreciate kind words that lift our failing spirits, and half hours spent thanking people who have blessed us or encouraging them when they hurt mean so much.

Inspiration from Tommy
"Take a look at all of the lives that nourish you during the day; let those people know what it means to you. It will certainly mean a lot to them."

(♩) **The Plan/Action Steps**
1. For a half hour, list people who have encouraged you during difficult times. Think about what they did for you and how they did it.
2. Then use a half hour occasionally to thank people who have made a positive difference in your life and/or encourage people you know who are hurting. You might write a note, send a book, or give a gift card.

Personal Action Plan #26

Reading Assignment—Chapter 26: Serve in a Loving Church

◑ **Half-Hour Power Principle:** *Help make your church relevant.*
Amid so much discussion about what the church is and does, and the "secrets" of church growth, it's interesting that two essentials stand out: the movement of the Holy Spirit to tell the good news of the gospel, and the expression of love and grace to needy people. So each of us can find ways to help build the Lord's church using half hours intentionally.

Inspiration from Tommy
"Oh, how I love the *relevant,* local church—being the very body of the Lord Jesus in action."

◑ **The Plan/Action Steps**
1. Think about how you and others in your church might: pray every day; fast one day a week; ask God to send a revival; bring an unsaved person every Sunday morning; and tithe for a month.
2. Whether you are a pastor or a layperson, use at least a half hour to think about how God might use you to release resources He has stored in the body of Christ.
3. Spend a half hour thinking about down-and-out and hurting people and how you might help them in tangible, practical ways through care and compassion. Then use half hours to start taking action!

Personal Action Plan #27

Reading Assignment—Chapter 27: Spread the Gospel

◔ **Half-Hour Power Principle:** *Take opportunities to share God's love.*
God gives us daily, important divine appointments to help people get right with God. That's amazing, right? Yet it is easy to help meet people's physical needs but not talk about the gospel and Christ's love for them. Sometimes opportunities to spread the gospel arise at unexpected moments, and we need to be spiritually sensitive enough to recognize them and respond with love and biblical truth.

Inspiration from Tommy
"As followers of Jesus we are commanded to share the good news of our salvation with others. If we are willing, He will give us the opportunities—those divine appointments.... God can do the things you would never expect if you're open to being used when He so chooses."

◔ **The Plan/Action Steps**
1. During a half hour, reflect on the quotation above, then prayerfully consider these questions:
   - Why is it important to share the gospel?
   - What might God have you be and/or do to prepare yourself to be more sensitive to His leading?
   - Which false beliefs about God and/or yourself (i.e., ones not matching with God's Word) might be hindering you from sharing the gospel? (Example: "I don't know enough about the Bible.") Pray about this.
   - Which followers of Jesus might join with you in spreading the gospel? (Remember, the Evil One will try to stop you from doing this, and we each need like-minded followers of Jesus to stand with us.)

Personal Action Plan #28

Reading Assignment—Chapter 28: Give Extravagantly

⚙ **Half-Hour Power Principle:** *Practice giving until you get really good at it.*
When you give someone a gift, you communicate that the recipient is being thought about, is cared for, and is important enough to justify the effort and resources you poured into that gift. Your gift may be a material possession or your best thinking on solving a problem, developing a creative concept, or refining a plan. Just think about all the different kinds of gifts you might give to people— family members, strangers, neighbors, friends! The opportunities are endless.

Inspiration from Tommy
"Expressions of care and compassion can make a big difference in [a] person's life. And it takes only a few minutes."

⚙ **The Plan/Action Steps**
1. Invest a half hour in thinking about ways in which you might give people gifts—and what those gifts might be.
2. Using half hours, start distributing those gifts joyfully and thankfully to people.

Personal Action Plan #29

Reading Assignment—Chapter 29: Take Kingdom Risks

◯ **Half-Hour Power Principle:** *Take a risk for God—what could be safer?*
Will you set aside a half hour to discern whether or not to pursue an audacious outcome meant to advance God's kingdom? Many people fear to take risks, including those who rely on faith in God—who He is and His promises.

God often uses our courageous risk taking to bless other people—and us too! Often He gives us specific ideas and passion for particular projects, and we have opportunities to take risks in pursuing them. Some risks are small. Others are large.

Inspiration from Tommy
"Take a risk; invest a half hour in something that might generate tremendous returns—or nothing at all.... Use your half hours to risk wisely, and you'll make a real difference in your world."

◯ **The Plan/Action Steps**
1. Which opportunities came to mind relating to risk taking for God's kingdom? Ask God to place inspired ideas in your mind and opportunities before you in your everyday life.
   - Write these down without worrying about how silly or impossible they may seem.
   - Pray over your list, seeking God's wisdom.
   - Seeking guidance from the Holy Spirit, discern whether or not to pursue particular risks. (Pray. Do Bible study. Seek wise and godly counsel. Pay attention to what God communicates to you.)
   - As the Holy Spirit prompts, pursue at least one risky opportunity soon.

Personal Action Plan #30

Reading Assignment—Chapter 30: Act!

🔔 **Half-Hour Power Principle:** *Follow God into His amazing adventure for you.*

Many biblical characters took action, faithfully trusting God and using opportunities to do the unexpected. Your willingness to allow God to use your half hours may take you on a journey that pushes you out of your comfort zone and ultimately bears tremendous fruit.

What may God want you to try? How will He turn your half hours into actions that further His kingdom?

To fulfill God's purpose in your life, you must take action—and possibly risks. Knowing which risks to take is between you and God, who will provide guidance if you provide the ear and the effort.

Inspiration from Tommy

"If you accept the fact that God created us to be agents of transformation and realize that every day He gives us opportunities to change the world…, then the half hours that you have to work with can produce great outcomes."

🔔 **The Plan/Action Steps**

1. Ponder the relationship between waiting on the Lord, preparing for action, and acting at the appropriate moment.
   - When have you waited and taken no action? prepared to act at the appropriate moment? taken action that involved risk to further God's kingdom?

2. Every day write down which course(s) of action required you to take meaningful risk. (If your list is blank, evaluate whether you trust God and/or are truly open to personal growth.)

3. From now on, spend half hours taking action and intelligent risks… and experiencing the power of a half hour!

SMALL-GROUP STUDY GUIDE

Note to Leader and Participants:

In conjunction with the theme of this book, this small-group study guide is designed for a group that meets with a limited time frame—for example, perhaps during a one-hour breakfast or lunch slot. The group should be able to discuss the material adequately in—of course—a half hour!

SESSION 1: THE POWER OF A HALF HOUR TO IMPACT YOUR LIFE (INTRODUCTION, CHAPTERS 1–2)

(Note: Your group may not cover all of the following questions. Feel free to choose which questions to address during this half hour.)

1. A thirty-minute period of time is long enough to accomplish positive or negative consequences.
   - Briefly describe a time when thirty minutes of your time created consequences you will never forget.
   - What do your answers reveal about what can happen during a thirty-minute period?
2. Why is it important to use small increments of time well, not just longer ones?
3. How might using half hours make a positive difference in your life?
4. Which step(s) are you already taking—or thinking about—to be intentional with your half hours every day? (Be sure to include fun activities such as reading, playing with a child, snuggling with your spouse, encouraging a friend.)

Pray

As your meeting ends, pray that God will honor your future half hours and bring blessings to you and those around you. Also ask God to help you immediately plan intentional half hours before your next group meeting.

Session 2: The Power of a Half Hour
to Chart Your Path (Chapters 3–5)

(Note: Your group may not cover all of the following questions. Feel free to choose which questions to address during this half-hour discussion.)

1. Would you say that you know and pursue God's unique purpose and vision for you—a special thing He needs done on earth? Why or why not?
   - How might spending specific half-hour sessions in prayer asking God to make your path clear benefit you—and those around you?
2. To what extent have external influences (family members, peers, media, and so on) and internal pressures (bad thinking, out-of-control feelings) shaped your values?
3. Take a few moments to write your bucket list: things you'd like to do and places you'd like to visit before you die. Then discuss them. What really motivates you? What's really important to you? (Be as honest as you can.)
4. Why is it important for us to take our God-given gifts (including skills, talents, abilities) seriously and refine them?
   - What types of things can we do to hone our spiritual gifts once we discover what they are (i.e., observe and imitate others who possess similar capacities)?
   - How might we each use a series of half hours to help other people identify and mature their gifts?

Pray

As your meeting ends, pray that God will honor your future half hours and bring blessings to you and those around you. Also ask God to aid you in recognizing and pursuing God's purpose and vision for you and in better identifying and maturing your God-given gifts. Finally, pray that each of you will continue to use your half hours well and regularly.

SESSION 3: THE POWER OF A HALF HOUR TO STRENGTHEN YOUR FAITH (CHAPTERS 6–8)

(Note: Your group may not cover all of the following questions. Feel free to choose which questions to address during this half-hour discussion.)

1. When you hear the phrase *being a genuine follower of Christ,* what immediately comes to mind? Why?
   - What has God already done to demonstrate His desire to be in a personal, growing relationship with us?

2. What might you change in your daily routine in order to spend thirty minutes alone with God and keep developing and practicing personal spiritual habits?
   - What makes the Bible so different from other books?

3. When you read "I treat prayer as if I am spending time with my best friend," what did you think? Why?
   - What can we do to prepare ourselves to enter God's holy presence?
   - What role does the Holy Spirit have in our prayer life?

4. How important is it for us to be still before God and listen for what He desires to tell us?
   - Why is being still so difficult for many people?

Pray

Pray for one another, that each of you will be motivated to spend thirty minutes alone with God regularly and receive His blessings. Ask God to deepen your prayer life: to help you remain still before Him and listen to what He communicates to you.

SESSION 4: THE POWER OF A HALF HOUR TO BUILD YOUR CHARACTER (CHAPTERS 9–14)

(Note: Your group may not cover all of the following questions. Feel free to choose which questions to address during this half-hour discussion.)

1. How do the following tips help to develop a spirit of humility within us?
   - Using phrases such as *It was my pleasure.*
   - Complimenting and giving credit to other coworkers.
   - Really listening to coworkers, friends, and family members.
   - Admitting when we are wrong.
   - Embracing someone else's competing, better idea and supporting it.

2. What would happen if you walked into a room and stated, "There you are" rather than "Here I am"?

3. What does God say about unforgiveness, including how it affects our prayers? (Before any more discussion, take a moment to reflect on whether there is anyone you owe an apology. Then after this session write a letter asking for forgiveness—and mail/e-mail it!)

4. Why are the following such important half-hour activities?
   - Ask someone we've wronged to forgive us.
   - Improve the attitudes we embrace every day.
   - Express gratitude to people around us, helping them to feel valued and loved.
   - Thank God for what He has done, is doing, and will do in our lives.
   - Slow down enough to be still in God's presence in order to make sense of the turbulence and challenges we face, reflect on what really matters, and know what God calls us to do and to be every day.

Pray

As your meeting ends, ask God to guide you into humility and to give you the strength and courage to both ask for forgiveness and to forgive others rather than building up walls of bitterness. Be sure to thank God for His many blessings and for the motivation to keep using half hours effectively.

SESSION 5: THE POWER OF A HALF HOUR
TO ADVANCE YOUR DREAMS (CHAPTERS 15–19)

(Note: Your group may not cover all of the following questions. Feel free to choose which questions to address during this half-hour discussion.)

1. In what way(s) have your inner dreams—the one(s) God birthed within you—changed since you were young?
   - Why is it often easy to abandon our passion—what really drives us—and settle for much less?
   - What difference should it make that God loves to fulfill in us the dreams He birthed?

2. When you read chapter 16, which emphasized the necessary hard work of preparing for success, what came to mind? Why?
   - Why are many people unwilling to work hard at tasks in order to fulfill their unique calling from God?
   - Discuss the three types of preparation—spiritual, mental, physical—and why preparing during half hours will help you maximize your potential and ultimately improve your chances of success.

3. Describe a day when you set aside a little time to activate your creativity. What happened, and what creativity might you be able to express during future half hours?

4. Why is hope so vital to our lives, and what three strategies does Tommy use to energize hope?

5. According to Romans 5:3–5, what is the true foundation for unshakable hope, and why do so many people try to find hope other ways?

Pray

Pray about what you discussed today, thanking God for helping you to learn new ways of thinking. Thank Him also for enabling you to learn more about Him and His relationship with you.

SESSION 6: THE POWER OF A HALF HOUR
TO IMPROVE YOUR RELATIONSHIPS (CHAPTERS 20–25)

(Note: Your group may not cover all of the following questions. Feel free to choose which questions to address during this half-hour discussion.)

1. What are some practical ways in which we can use half hours as a resource to share Jesus's love: to build up other people, make their lives better, and encourage them?

2. Describe a time when someone invested half hours—of energy, ideas, commitment, face time—in befriending you or someone you love.

3. Whether you are married, have been married, or have observed the marriages of others, answer this question: why can regular thirty-minute investments of time benefit a married couple?

   • Why is protecting time for one another so difficult for many married couples?

4. Describe family relationships you have experienced. How would the wise use of some half hours make your family life more productive and fulfilling?

   • Why is it so important for family members to listen to what is being said—directly or indirectly—and to be fully present to one another?

   • Which specific half-hour activities do you share with family members—or with friends if your family lives far away—and what extra half hours might you devote to them?

5. Which hurting person(s) might you help/encourage in your community in half-hour blocks of time? (Remember, we all need help sometimes in this life!)

Pray

Pray about what you learned during this session, thanking God for stimulating new ways of thinking and more understanding about Him. In what way(s) is this book guiding you into new thoughts about God and His relationship with you?

SESSION 7: THE POWER OF A HALF HOUR TO CHANGE YOUR WORLD (CHAPTERS 26–30)

(Note: Your group may not cover all of the following questions. Feel free to choose which questions to address during this half-hour discussion.)

1. What are some characteristics of a relevant church, and in what specific ways can you meet the needs of unsaved people in your community, then invite them to be saved?

2. Why do investments of thirty minutes to demonstrate care and compassion to needy people make such an impact?

3. In light of the truth that God gives us divine appointments every day, how do we...

   • become more sensitive to God's leading?

   • meet spiritual needs at the same time we meet physical needs?

   • use half hours to share the life-changing Gospel message?

   • overcome reasons for not sharing Christ with people?

4. What need(s), even within your group today, might be met if you are willing to use a half hour to take a wise risk and see what God will do?

Pray

Express gratefulness to God for what you have learned through group discussion. Pray for one another, that each of you will continue to use half hours regularly and effectively. Ask God to use you in special ways—within the church and your local community, among needy people who need Jesus. Commit yourselves to be still before Him and use the gifts He has given you to benefit other people.

Notes

1. *Building Personal Strength Blog,* "The Best of Harvey Mackay—17 Great Quotes," July 15, 2011, www.buildingpersonalstrength.com/2011/07/best-of -harvey-mackay-17-great-quotes.html.

2. This is a true story, but the name has been changed to protect the identity of the individual who experienced this episode.

3. Ezekiel 34:21.

4. Matthew 28:20, KJV.

5. See 1 Samuel 3:1–19; 1 Samuel 17; Acts 18:24–28; Matthew 16:15–19; Acts 26:2–29.

6. See James 4:8.

7. See Romans 8:26.

8. Lou Holtz, quoted in George Barna and Bill Dallas, *Master Leaders* (Carol Stream, IL: Tyndale, 2010), 188.

9. See Proverbs 18:12; Matthew 23:12; 1 Peter 5:5.

10. *Acton Institute Power Blog,* "Leading by Example with Humility," blog entry by Ray Nothstine, March 28, 2011, http://blog.acton.org/archives/22472 -leading-by-example-with-humility.html.

11. The Scott Hamilton CARES Initiative, "About Scott Hamilton," http://www .clevelandclinic.org/cancer/scottcares/scott/about.asp.

12. John C. Maxwell, *Developing the Leader Within You* (Nashville: Thomas Nelson, 1993), 98.

13. Matthew 25:35–36, NLT.

14. Howard Bingham and Max Wallace, *Muhammad Ali's Greatest Fight: Cassius Clay vs the United States of America* (New York: Evans and Company, 2008), 138.

15. See Jeremiah 29:11.

16. See Job 11:18; 13:15; Psalms 31:24; 119:43; 147:11; Jeremiah 29:11; Romans 5:1–5; 8:24; 15:4; Ephesians 1:18; Colossians 1:5; 1 Thessalonians 2:19; Hebrews 3:6.

17. See Genesis 12:1–3.

18. George Barna; *The Seven Faith Tribes: Who They Are, What They Believe, and Why They Matter* (Carol Stream, IL: Tyndale, 2010) 149–67.

19. Paul Tillich, quoted in Malcolm Duncan, *Risk Takers* (Oxford: Monarch Books, 2013), 29.

20. Jimmy Carter, *The Virtues of Aging* (New York: Ballantine, 1998), 87.

About the Author

Tommy Barnett is the senior pastor of Phoenix First Assembly of God in Phoenix, Arizona. The church is known as "The Church with a Heart" because of its more than 275 active outreach ministries.

Tommy Barnett's life is an example of commitment to reaching out to others and training leaders in church growth and outreach, and for this he has become known as a "pastor's pastor." His tenacity and refusal to step down from a challenge have inspired him to take unprecedented leaps of faith in ministry and, by example, to encourage pastors and leaders around the world to spread the love of God and change the lives of many through a relentless spirit of servanthood.

Following in his father's example of generosity, Tommy Barnett became devoted to reaching the lost and healing the hurting, and began his ministry at age sixteen. His early background in music and global evangelism laid the foundation for his high-impact, soul-winning ministry.

Before moving to Phoenix First, he pastored Westside Assembly of God in Davenport, Iowa. In just a few years, the church grew from seventy-six people to more than four thousand members, becoming the fastest-growing church in America. The rapid growth attracted global attention and quickly became an example of new revival in America's local churches. It also set the stage for what would happen in Arizona when he became the pastor of Phoenix First Assembly in 1979.

Under his leadership for over three decades, Tommy Barnett has guided Phoenix First Assembly into an era of phenomenal revival. Thousands of people of all ages and backgrounds in the community have committed their lives to Christ every year. His innovative approach of utilizing the creative arts and compassionate ministries to present the gospel and reach out to the poor and the hurting have become signature components of his ministry.

Tommy Barnett and his son Matthew copastor the Los Angeles Dream Center, where the former Queen of Angels Hospital and Angelus Temple have become the center of inner-city outreach in the metropolitan area. The LA Dream Center has inspired the development of nearly two hundred additional Dream Centers around the world, and Tommy Barnett recently launched the New York Dream Center. He has also been appointed chancellor of Grand Canyon University and, later, Southeastern University.

He considers his greatest success to be his three children, who all love God and are actively involved in ministry. Kristie is an outstanding leader who speaks at Women's Conferences worldwide. Matthew is pastor of the Los Angeles Dream Center. And Luke is the lead pastor of Phoenix First Assembly, where under his outstanding leadership the church is experiencing great growth. This has allowed Pastor Barnett the time to speak internationally at churches and conferences.

His annual Pastors and Leaders School has gathered more than 200,000 leaders over thirty-three years to train and equip the next generation of pastors and ministry leaders to carry on the work of the ministry. Tommy Barnett's ministry has influenced many leaders, including many high-profile ministers who call him their pastor.

He is a highly sought-after conference and evangelistic speaker, recently partnering with Joyce Meyer to share the gospel with more than 400,000 people in India. He has authored several previous books, including *Multiplication, Hidden Power, Enlarge Your Circle of Love, Reaching Your Dreams,* and *Miracle in the House.*